How To Talk About Jesus Without Freaking Out

Jim & Karen Covell
Victorya Michaels Rogers

Multnomah Publishers   *Sisters, Oregon*

HOW TO TALK ABOUT JESUS WITHOUT FREAKING OUT
published by Multnomah Publishers, Inc.

©2000 by Jim Covell, Karen Covell, and Victorya Michaels Rogers
International Standard Book Number: 1-57673-737-3
Scripture quotations are from: *Holy Bible,* New Living Translation ©1996.
Used by permission of Tyndale House Publishers, Inc. All rights reserved.

Also quoted:
The Holy Bible, New International Version (NIV) © 1973, 1984 by International Bible
Society, used by permission of Zondervan Publishing House.
All Scripture used in "The Bridge" is from the NIV.
New American Standard Bible (NASB) © 1960, 1977, 1995 by the Lockman Foundation.
Used by permission.

Multnomah is a trademark of Multnomah Publishers, Inc., and
is registered in the U.S. Patent and Trademark Office.
The colophon is a trademark of Multnomah Publishers, Inc.

Printed in the United States of America

For information:
MULTNOMAH PUBLISHERS, INC.•POST OFFICE BOX 1720•SISTERS, OREGON 97759

Library of Congress Cataloging-in-Publication Data
Covell, Jim
How to talk about Jesus without freaking out/by Jim Covell, Karen Covell, and Victorya
Michaels Rogers.   p.cm.
Includes bibliographical references.
ISBN 1-57673-737-3 (pbk)
1. Witness bearing (Christianity I. Covell, Karen. II Rogers, Victorya Michaels. III. Title.
BV4520 .C675 2000   248' .5—dc21   00-008423

00 01 02 03 04 05 — 10 9 8 7 6 5 4 3 2 1 0

"This book is practical, challenging, and compelling. It contains vital information that will help today's Christians effectively share their faith in the twenty-first century."

JOSH MCDOWELL
BESTSELLING AUTHOR AND FOUNDER, JOSH MCDOWELL MINISTRY

"Jim, Karen, and Victorya are in the front lines of spiritual influence. They are helping to reach the inhabitants of a 'hidden people group'—those in Hollywood—that has the potential to help reach the entire world for Christ. Their book, *How To Talk About Jesus without Freaking Out,* is a must read."

DR. BILL BRIGHT
FOUNDER AND PRESIDENT, CAMPUS CRUSADE FOR CHRIST INTERNATIONAL

"My friends Jim and Karen Covell and Victorya Rogers have for years helped many in Hollywood become bolder in sharing their faith. In a winsome, inspirational, and practical way, their book challenges the concerns and hesitations we have about witnessing. They help us to become more alert to the many exciting encounters God arranges in our lives every day, and they give us the tools we need to build our confidence in sharing the Good News. Their enthusiasm is contagious!"

NANCY STAFFORD
ACTRESS AND HOST OF TELEVISION'S *MAIN FLOOR*

"It has been my privilege this past year to get to know the authors of this book. I can tell you from firsthand exposure that their passion for Christ and for sharing Him with the world is both genuine and winsome. It is my pleasure to share them now with the world through this, their first book"

KEN GIRE
AUTHOR OF *INTIMATE MOMENTS WITH THE SAVIOR,*
WINDOWS OF THE SOUL, AND *THE REFLECTIVE LIFE*

"From the first page to the last, *How to Talk About Jesus without Freaking Out* is a book about doing, about acting, about actually being the witness we are all called to be. Jim, Karen, and Victorya have honed their skills and developed their talent in the nation's most difficult witnessing field—Hollywood. Like Paul in Athens, they have not been cowed by the culture around them. Like Paul, they have figured out how to talk to family, friends, business colleagues, and total strangers about the gospel. You can have the benefit of their experience, and your witness will change dramatically as a result."

HUGH HEWITT
COHOST, *LIFE AND TIMES TONIGHT,* PBS TELEVISION (LOS ANGELES AFFILIATE) AND AUTHOR OF *THE EMBARRASSED BELIEVER* AND *SEARCHING FOR GOD IN AMERICA*

"This book is for the 90 percent of believers who have never presented the full gospel to an unbeliever. The authors learned the techniques they present in the often hostile environment of Hollywood, where I minister. If these techniques work in Hollywood, they will work anywhere. And I can assure you, they do work in Hollywood!"

LARRY W. POLAND, PH.D
CHAIRMAN AND CEO, MASTERMEDIA INTERNATIONAL

"Most believers want to share their faith, but don't know how. Jim, Karen, and Victorya have produced a myriad of useful insights on evangelism that are bathed in personal experience and are biblically based. They hit the nail on the head with their section on using your personal testimony, which is the most important, persuasive tool a believer possesses—'I was blind but now I see!'"

TIM TIMMONS
SENIOR PASTOR, NEW COMMUNITY CHURCH, AUTHOR OF *CALL IT LOVE OR CALL IT QUITS* AND *HOOKED ON LIFE*

"In a day and age when being spiritual is popular but being a Christian isn't, this book is a perfect evangelistic tool! I applaud the way it breaks down the 'Christian-ese' and helps a person deliver the good news of Jesus."

HOLLY McCLURE
NATIONALLY SYNDICATED MOVIE CRITIC AND RADIO TALK SHOW HOST

*We dedicate this book to all the people who have taken our class.
Thank you for your commitment to obey the Lord and
go out into all nations.
You have been an encouragement and
an inspiration to all three of us.*

Table of Contents

Acknowledgments

From All Three of Us

Most importantly, thank You, Jesus, for giving us the words and the passion to write this book. We love talking about You!

Many thanks to Ken Gire, Glen Evans, and Sandra Sterud, who gave us invaluable feedback on our first draft. We are forever indebted to Josh McDowell, Bill Bright, and Hugh Hewitt. Your hearts for reaching the world are contagious, and your support of our vision means more to us than you know.

We also appreciate so much the encouragement we received from Holly McClure, Nancy Stafford Myers, Dr. Larry Poland, and Tim Timmons.

Susan Wales, thank you for selflessly introducing us to Penny Whipps. Penny, you truly are our champion. Bill Jensen, thank you for believing in us. We love to hear your stories! Thank you so much to our fantastic editors, Jeff Gerke, Heather Kopp, and especially Judith St. Pierre.

We also thank all of our friends who read our drafts, prayed for us, and kept us going. And hats off to all of you who let us tell your story. You added infinite richness to the book.

From Jim and Karen

Victorya, three strands truly are stronger than two. We love you! We also believe this book never would have happened without Shelly Moore and our mighty prayer warriors. You know who you are. You have been our life support for the past year. The other Jim and Karen, thank you for being our devoted small group. Bill Spuck, thank you for your wise input. And Genesis, you are the best Sunday school class in the world.

Our families—every single one of you—deserve more than

thanks for your unconditional love and support. And a final thank you to our wonder boys, Christopher and Cameron, the joys of our lives. We pray that you'll grow up to be "mighty warrior attack sheep"! Oh, and Vic, isn't it great that *we* never freak out...?

From Victorya

Jim and Karen Covell, it has been so exciting and such a privilege to work with you on this book from our hearts.

I deeply appreciate all the love, prayers, and encouragement from my wonderful husband, Will, as well as from my parents, Curtis and Sandra Sterud; my in-laws, Bob and Pat Rogers; Grandma and Grandpa Sterud; my brother David Sterud and sister Teri Rippeon; plus the rest of my family and friends who hung in there with me and kept cheering me on. I love you all so much.

Lastly, thanks to my other faithful cheerleaders: Vic Costa, Prescilla Davis, Christine Devine, Kellie Stade, and our HHBC Akins/Talley Flock.

Introduction

About fifteen years ago, Karen was managing a singing group at a prestigious Los Angeles club. When she sat down to schedule their rehearsals, the male singer, Pendleton, suggested that Wednesdays would be a good night to practice. Karen was a fairly new Christian and had just committed to attend a Bible study on Wednesday nights. Without thinking, she said she couldn't meet on that night of the week because of her Bible study.

"A Bible study?" Pen said. "Is that nun practice? Well, we don't want to get in the way of nun practice, do we? By all means, let's pick another night."

Every week from then on, Karen would hear some comment about her "nun practice." She laughed about it, but she was very embarrassed. She vowed never again to tell anyone in her business about her Christian life. It just wasn't worth it.

Chickens Anonymous

Does this scenario look familiar? When you find yourself in a situation in which you ought to be telling someone about Jesus, do you freeze up? Have you had a bad experience when you've tried to talk about your faith? We're here to tell you that we all feel hesitation, trepidation, or even total panic when it comes to talking about Jesus. It's natural.

Nevertheless, we know we're supposed to do it. We know God wants to use us to reach out in His name, and we know the person we're talking to needs what we have. But we're just so scared. Stuck between responsibility and fear is not a good place to be. In the end we may keep quiet, let the moment slip away, and then beat ourselves up about it for days—or even longer.

If talking about Jesus is so important, why do we do it so rarely and only hesitantly? Why do we sit next to that coworker day in and day out, yet never engage in that desperately important conversation about Jesus Christ? How many times do we try to muster the courage to bring up the subject with Dad or Aunt Lorraine? Why do we come to the edge of the diving board, only to lose our nerve and climb down the ladder, humiliated?

It must be because we're at risk when we talk about our faith. We put ourselves out on a limb, spiritually and emotionally, and we become vulnerable—primarily to rejection. And none of us wants to be rejected, especially for our faith.

For years, the three of us have taught classes to help professional Christian entertainers overcome their fears about sharing their faith. The class, called *How to Talk about Jesus without Freaking Out*, is nicknamed "Chickens Anonymous." All of us feel we need a twelve-step program to get over the fear of sharing our faith.

We work in Hollywood, the entertainment capital of the world, where believing in Jesus is considered the equivalent of a box office flop, and talking about Him is even worse. But we can tell you that rich and famous people need Jesus Christ just as much as your family member, friend, or hairdresser. Because of our experiences in this spiritually unreceptive place, we can teach you ways to be effective when you're asked to give an account for the hope that is in you.

You will also benefit personally from talking to others about Jesus. Do you know that talking about Jesus will actually help you grow in your faith? One little verse in the Bible has changed our whole perspective on how to live out our Christian faith as effective messengers of truth:

> *I pray that you may be active in sharing your faith, so that you will have a full understanding of every good thing we have in Christ.*
>
> PHILEMON 6, NIV

How do we experience all the good things that the Lord has to offer and live a life that bears ripe fruit? We talk about Jesus!

I'm No Billy Graham

Witnessing. Ugh! The W word. Few words strike so much fear into the hearts of otherwise bold believers. Research has shown that getting up in front of an audience is the number one fear in America. Fear of death is second! We would venture to guess that if they added sharing one's Christian faith to the equation, it would be a strong contender for first place.

So what does it mean to witness to someone about Jesus? The *New Webster's Dictionary* defines a witness as: "One who personally sees or observes anything; that which furnishes evidence or proof; a testimony." A witness, then, is just someone who tells what he knows or has seen.

Witnessing is not the same as evangelism. Webster defines evangelism as: "The fervent, zealous preaching or promulgation of the gospel." That's what we're afraid of, isn't it? Getting out there and preaching like a fanatic.

The Bible doesn't command us all to be evangelists. Jesus told His disciples that they were to be His *witnesses* (Acts 1:8). Some people have the spiritual gift of evangelism. If you have that gift, that's wonderful. Go for it! But if you don't, don't panic. You probably haven't been called to go out and preach the gospel to the multitudes. Neither do you have to be a zealot, with all the negative baggage that term carries.

But you *do* have to be ready and willing to tell what you know or what you have seen about Jesus. You have to be a witness.

> *Always be prepared to give an answer to everyone*
> *who asks you to give the reason for the hope that you have.*
> *But do this with gentleness and respect.*
> 1 PETER 3:15B, NIV

All God expects is for you to understand your own experience of God through Jesus and to be able to explain it when it is appropriate or when you are asked.

This Little Light of Mine

This should be a great relief to those of you who take all the unsaved people in the world on your shoulders and feel personally responsible to lead them all to the Lord.

This will not be a relief, however, to those of you who have decided not to talk about Jesus to anyone because you feel that it's not one of the gifts God gave you. This is also less than thrilling for those of you who know you should tell others about your faith but have decided that you can't until you have had more Bible training, done more memorizing, earned more theological degrees, or stopped making so many mistakes.

From this moment on, those arguments will not work. Witnessing—telling other people about Jesus—is not just something for professional clergy and the spiritual elite. Nor is it optional. The minute someone learns that you're a Christian, you have become a witness. Sorry, there are no secret agents for the Lord. One reason God didn't beam you up into heaven the moment you were

14

saved is that He wanted to have a representative right where you are. You're His ambassador to the "nation" that is your social circle.

The good news is that effective witnessing isn't very hard. As we saw in the case of Karen and Pendleton, even the slightest comment identifying you as belonging to Jesus sets you apart from the world. You are a city set on a hill, a candle burning in the dark. Though the darkness may not like your light, it certainly can't ignore you. And guess what? The darkness cannot overpower the light (John 1:5).

What's hard about witnessing is being willing to stand up and be counted as a Christian. Take it from us, we know there are times and places in which it is very difficult to do that. When you know you're going to be ridiculed, ostracized, passed over, or marginalized, it's a daunting prospect.

Yet you wouldn't have picked up this book if there weren't something in you that wants to stand up for Jesus, whatever the cost. It is for you, brave reader, that we have written this book.

In these pages, we'll give you a few tips about how to talk about Jesus without panicking. We'll also give you simple, practical tools to help you talk about Jesus without being pushy, rude, or obnoxious. So stop freaking out!

Who Are We? Jim Covell

I grew up in an abnormal, politically incorrect family—Christian and functional. I learned about Jesus at an early age and have had the privilege of following Him throughout my life.

I met Karen, my wife, while studying music composition at the University of Southern California. There at USC, God was preparing me to work in the most influential mission field in the world—the American media. I am a film and television composer, a husband, and a father of two wonder boys. I've found that as a composer I can have a positive influence on the producers and directors with whom

I work—and even on the content of the music I score—just by being available to God's leading.

Who Are We? Karen Covell

My family went to church every week but never talked about God, let alone Jesus. We were an artistic family, so when I went to college, it was with a singular focus: to take over the theater world. But I didn't know what God had in store for me.

During my freshman year as a theater-producing major at USC, my roommate started talking to me about God. Our discussions eventually led me to become a Christian. God then began to show me that His plan for me involved much more than just theater.

For almost two decades I have been a producer in the television industry. I have created TV movies, produced children's video series, and worked with a host of Christians and non-Christians. Yet my fulfillment comes not from my career, but from my ministry, my relationships with the Lord and with Jim and our two boys, Christopher and Cameron, and from telling others about Jesus—something I never would have even been capable of imagining years ago.

Who Are We? Victorya Rogers

In the 1990s, I was an agent in Hollywood. I represented a wide range of people for television and feature films: producers, writers, directors, actors, editors, cinematographers, sound-mixers, stuntmen, designers, and makeup artists. My clients have won awards across the board—everything from Emmys to Oscars. It was an exciting career.

But nothing can lift me higher than speaking to someone about Jesus. In Hollywood, it's considered politically correct to be "religious" about something—even something spiritual. But it's definitely not acceptable to worship Jesus Christ. Getting past my fears has been life changing and quite thrilling.

At night, while still an agent, I earned a master of theology degree at Fuller Theological Seminary, and I became an ordained minister. Now I live in Oklahoma with my Christian husband, Will Rogers, who is every bit as amazing as the "famous" Will Rogers was.

The Rest of Karen's Story

Soon after the singing group parted ways, Karen got a phone call from Pendleton. He began the conversation with, "You know that nun practice of yours?"

This will never die! "Yes."

"Well," he said, "I'd like to get together to talk about that."

She anxiously drove over to his house. They sat in her car while Pen explained that he had grown up in the church but had gotten away from God. His life hadn't turned out the way he had expected, and he thought it might be time to get his spiritual affairs in order.

Karen told him about her personal relationship with Christ, and she got the incredible privilege of praying with Pen as he received Christ into his life right there in her car.

She realized then that Pen's jabs at her "nun practice" had not been meant for her at all. It was his own spiritual struggle coming out as his heart was convicted. He could handle his conflict only by poking fun at the source of his conviction. And yet, the very person he chose to talk to about Jesus was Karen—who went to nun practice!

By the way, today Pendleton is an incredible youth pastor and performing artist who records praise CDs and leads many young people to Christ.

PART I

Freaking Out

CHAPTER ONE

Excuses, Excuses

When the Holy Spirit has come upon you,
you will receive power and will tell people about me everywhere—
in Jerusalem, throughout Judea, in Samaria, and
to the ends of the earth.

ACTS 1:8

Jim Says: I was grounded in my faith by the time I was in junior high. I knew that my commitment was based on truth, not only because I had grown up in a Christian home with great role models, but also because I had looked into the facts of the Bible on my own and had come to my own understanding of who God is.

By my sophomore year of high school, however, I hadn't had many opportunities to share my faith, and so witnessing hadn't become a natural part of my life. I was following God, but not thinking much about witnessing to others.

One day I was driving my dad's sports car. My friend Rick was in the passenger seat, and my new driver's license was in my pocket—life was good. In midconversation, Rick turned to me and said in all seriousness, "Jim, you seem different than our other friends. You're so happy all the time and seem to handle life really well. What makes you like that?"

Suddenly all of my confidence vanished. I had no idea what to say. The few words I got out were empty and meaningless: "Um, well, I don't know. That's just the way I am, I guess." In my head I said, *He doesn't want to hear about God. He'll think it's so stupid. Maybe I can just change the conversation. I know I have to say something. But...*I changed the topic.

To this day, I have not forgotten Rick and his searching question that I never answered. I still wonder what happened to him. I pray that he found someone else who was more prepared to tell him about Jesus than I was. I determined then and there that I would never miss a divine opportunity like that again.

I'm Afraid I'll Fail

Fear of failure is universal. Talking about Jesus is taking a risk—and risk, by definition, involves the chance of failure. The thing to remember is that the outcome of a discussion about Jesus is not up to you.

Isn't that reassuring? We get so stressed out with performance anxiety that we forget we're only the messengers. You may think it's all up to you to persuade someone to come to Christ, when in reality it's up to God, who has strategically placed you in this specific situation and chosen to use you with this person—maybe even in spite of yourself. All you have to do is just show up and open your mouth.

It is easy to conclude that a witnessing encounter is a "failure" if the person to whom you are witnessing doesn't end the conversation by falling to his knees and asking Jesus into his heart.[1] But this is only a failure in your eyes. If you were obedient to speak the words God gave you to say, then that encounter was a success. God used you to deliver to that person the message He wanted him to hear. What happens after that is up to God.

Ever notice the effect of one pebble tossed into a still lake? The ripples cause change throughout the entire body of water. When you drop pebbles of truth in the water of someone's life, God takes care of the ripple effect. That person is responding to the Lord, not to you, even if he happens to be directing his reaction at you. Sometimes the messenger does get shot. But God gives you a bulletproof vest. You may get bruised, but you'll survive.

You never fail when you say something good or truthful about your Lord and Savior. The only failure in sharing your faith is not to share your faith at all.

Dr. Bill Bright, founder of Campus Crusade for Christ, defines witnessing as "taking the initiative to share Christ, in the power of the Holy Spirit, and leaving the results to God."[2] This is a perfect example of the Trinity at work in your life. You just bring it up—drop that pebble into the still water of a lost soul—and your part is done! You may still be called upon to act as God's spokesperson, but if so, your role will have changed. Then you're the *intermediary* between that person and God.

That is so freeing for us. It means we aren't the ones doing the converting. That's God's job. We only have to take the initiative. The pressure is off; the awkwardness is gone. How can you fail at witnessing if it is God's job to persuade someone? If you were a U.S. marshal, it would be your job to hand someone a court summons, but it would not be up to you to get that person to court. As soon as you've done your part, the matter is between that person and the law.

The Christian Businessmen's Association has another definition of witnessing: "Taking the initiative to help a person move one step closer in the process…not necessarily making 'a close.'" Doesn't that take the pressure off? "Making the close" is not the final test of whether you have witnessed successfully or been an effective ambassador for the Lord. If the people to whom we witness don't pray the "sinners' prayer" we are *not* failures. The final test of success is whether you have witnessed.

Looking at the New Testament, we see that in the days of the early church Christianity was spread through the power of the Holy Spirit. The same is true today! It is God who saves, not salesmen! All we have to do is believe, then ask the Holy Spirit for opportunities to share. When opportunities arrive, take the initiative, speak the truth, and trust the power of the Trinity to take care of the results.

The rest is up to God!

I Don't Want to Move to Africa!

Karen's greatest fear of becoming a Christian was that God would send her to a mission field in some third world country. Victorya had the same fear. It wasn't until we matured in our faith that we realized that we're all missionaries wherever God places us. A missionary is simply someone who shares his faith in Jesus to a world that is lost without Him. We think every church should post a large sign at the exit saying:

You are now entering your mission field.

We live and work in the entertainment industry in the famous city of Hollywood. But Hollywood is also our mission field. In fact, it is the world's most influential mission field because it impacts virtually every other mission field around the globe. If Washington, D.C., is the seat of power for the entire world, Hollywood is the seat of influence. An overseas missionary friend told us that he couldn't fathom how we could try to share our faith with people in Hollywood. "That must be the hardest place on earth!"

The truth is that the people here who do not know the Lord are as hungry for the truth as people in Kenya. The only difference is that some people here don't know they are starving. But they are, and deep inside they want to hear good news. As we work side by side with them and become their friends, we talk about Jesus and what we personally know about Him. In turn, people around us begin to learn who He is.

It may be that God *is* calling you to foreign missions. But it is more likely that He is calling you to home missions—to be a light in the darkness right around you (1 Corinthians 7:20–24). Don't assume that if you say yes to God, He will send you to the deepest, darkest part of Africa. Wherever God has placed you is your mission field. Start noticing the unsaved people you come in regular contact with right where you are.

The people you work with who do not know the Lord are hungry for truth. Maybe you're the only one around who can feed them. Author Max Lucado says:

> Do you ever get tired or bored with your work? Christ says turn your work into a ministry.... Don't let it be just a vocation. Reach out to people. Let your time at work be a source of joy and encouragement to others, and you'll find greater personal joy and satisfaction as well.[3]

That may be why you were given that position only temporarily. The same thing goes for the people you live next to. Maybe you're the reason that family moved in next door. Maybe you're the only one around who can offer them hope and life. God has prepared works for you to do (Ephesians 2:10). He moves His sowers into fields that are ready for the seed.

You have been commissioned to go out to all the nations. While that may include a foreign land, it most certainly includes your neighborhood, your workplace, your school grounds, and even your own home. People all around you are spiritually starving—and you have the bread of life! Once you realize that you are a missionary—no matter where you are—you'll talk about Jesus more comfortably and boldly, and you'll become a more effective witness.

Here's some advice that sounds obvious but is rarely heeded: You must share the gospel to people in their own language. Poor people lack many of the basic necessities of life, such as food, clothing, and shelter. When you help supply those needs, you may find that they are seeking God. Although the wealthy have more than enough money to meet their basic needs, they may be dying emotionally and spiritually. They need help with those needs as well. Suicide, violence, drug addiction, and alcoholism are rampant among the rich. Speak their language. Help them at the point of their felt needs. Then they may be willing to listen to what you have to say.

Henrietta Mears believed that whoever does not know Jesus is miserable! Rich and poor alike search for meaning and significance in any way they can. When one avenue disappoints, in despair people turn to something else. Each of us has unique needs, but we all need Christ.

So don't go pack your suitcase just yet. God probably wants you exactly where you are right now.

Karen Says: I once had a conversation on a plane with a Jewish man named Sam. He told me that the previous year his wife of fourteen years had had an affair. Sam was devastated. Unable to stand the pain, he left her. Within a couple of months he found another woman and, even though he was still married, began an affair with her. He rationalized the affair by saying that he truly believed God had "miraculously" brought him this woman and that the relationship was meant to be.

During our brief conversation, I was oversensitive to the fact

that Sam was Jewish and that he was at least starting to acknowledge God in his life. I became a wimp and wasn't as bold about the
truth of the gospel as I should have been.

I should have pointed out lovingly that he was just as wrong as
his wife had been. God would not bring him a soul mate while he was
still married, and he wasn't going to find fulfillment in a woman. That
could only come through Jesus, who was indeed his Messiah.

I didn't do any of that. However, I did take his card. A few days
later, as I wallowed in my guilt over a failed witnessing experience, I
pulled out Sam's card and wrote him a letter explaining the points of
the gospel that I had not brought up in our plane conversation.

I explained who God is. I told him that God's actions never con-
tradict His words to us in the Scriptures. I said that if Sam were really
seeking answers, emotional healing, and fulfillment, he would have to
find out about this Jesus, who was not only a Jew Himself, but the
only one through whom he could find true and lasting fulfillment.

I sent the letter off and prayed. (See the full text of this letter in
appendix A.)

But I'm Not Qualified!

"How can I get someone to pray the sinner's prayer or tell someone
that even though he's nice he's still going to hell? I can't. I just can't!
What if someone asks me something I don't know? What if they ask
me about Buddhists or transubstantiation or something? I'd need a
seminary degree to feel secure out there on the front lines. I didn't
even graduate from vacation Bible school!"

It's natural to feel intimidated about talking about Jesus. A certain
amount of stage fright or performance anxiety is to be expected. But
that doesn't give anyone permission not to do it.

God wants real people, not perfect ones. When you become a Christian you become a new creation (1 Corinthians 5:17), but that doesn't mean you are instantly perfect. Most of us will never be at a place in which we feel truly qualified to be a good witness. But if we are seeking after God with all our heart and soul and mind, God can use us mightily.

What God is looking for is someone who wants to be used by Him—a volunteer. All He asks of you is that you have a willing heart filled with love for your lost friend, family member, or acquaintance, and that you trust Him to use you as an instrument of peace in this world. Our hardest job is to get out of the way so that God can take over.

Just look at the Bible. God has always used ordinary people! "God deliberately chose things the world considers foolish in order to shame those who think they are wise. And he chose those who are powerless to shame those who are powerful" (1 Corinthians 1:27). The Gospels reveal how inadequate even Jesus' twelve disciples were, yet they changed the world. God wants to use you that same way, no matter who you are, what you do, or what you know.

You don't have to wait to have your life together and all your spiritual ducks in a row for God to use you. You don't have to understand the Torah, memorize the Sermon on the Mount, or point to theological degrees on your wall. Just be willing. Just show up.

Don't let what you consider a lack of expertise be the trick the enemy uses to keep you from opening your mouth. God will give you the words He wants you to say. Even if you appear to lose the battle, the words you say may eventually win the war.

But I'm Such a Bad Example!

"But I've messed up in front of my unbelieving friends. You don't know how bad. How can I possibly be used of God with them now?"

Guess what: No one is perfect. Solomon said, "There is not a single person in all the earth who is always good and never sins" (Ecclesiastes 7:20). And yes, you are going to sin, and most likely there will be people watching you do it. That doesn't mean it's okay to sin, nor does it get you out of your responsibility to bear witness to the hope that is in you. You will fail. Count on it. But sometimes how you handle your failures will be what makes the difference to unbelievers around you.

No one wants to be around someone perfect. All that does is make the imperfect one feel inferior. We're not saying to rush out and mess up in front of unbelievers. We're just making the point that we need to be transparent in order to be approachable by unbelievers. Let your friends see your disappointments and fears. Let coworkers see you wrestle with ethical issues and moral dilemmas. Let more people know your thoughts and even your questions about life and God. Your vulnerability is more important than your image.

Karen Says: Years ago I ran the office of a film festival. I hired Terry as the festival assistant. Though she had interviewed well, it wasn't long before the two of us began to clash. Terry began reacting with rage at work: Some days she slammed doors, yelled, cried, and ignored my requests.

I prayed for Terry and tried to talk with her, but nothing seemed to help. Finally one night she called to tell me that she had put up with more than her share of my demands and that she refused to do what I had asked. Jim happened to answer the phone. Terry was so rude to him that I said, "Tell her we've had enough. She must not want to work here, so tell her she doesn't need to come back." Terry said, "Fine," and slammed down the phone.

I just broke down and cried. I had really blown it. Not only had I lost my temper, but also I hadn't loved Terry unconditionally. Worse yet, I was so unprofessional that I had fired her through Jim! It was terrible.

In the ensuing weeks I left messages on Terry's answering machine saying that I was thinking of her, hoping that she had found another job, and praying that she was all right. She never returned my calls. After about three months, I left one last message, saying how sorry I was for my behavior and for the horrible way our relationship had ended.

The next day Terry called to say that she would meet with me. Our meeting was miraculous. We both cried. We talked about how much both of us had wanted our relationship to work. I learned that she had come from a frighteningly bad family and that she was still reeling from severe abuse and neglect. She had been a Christian as a child, but it had come to mean nothing to her because all she saw in her church and in her home were hypocrites.

Terry told me she greatly desired to get back into a relationship with the Lord. I got a chance to offer my support and prayers; I even offered to disciple her. We agreed to get together once a week. The following year she went to seminary. And despite my initial poor witness, Terry is now a certified pastor, counseling others who have gone down similar paths.

We're All Recovering Humans

You've seen the bumper sticker: Christians aren't perfect, just forgiven.

We all know the apostle Paul was a hero of the Christian faith. But what we need to remember is that he was Saul before he was Paul. Saul hated Christians and was responsible for murdering many of them, including Stephen. Look how Jesus forgave him and transformed him into a new creation.

King David plotted to have Bathsheba's husband killed so he could marry his widow. Yet God later accepted his repentance and declared that David was a "man after his own heart." Moses murdered an Egyptian and spent the following forty years in exile herding sheep. Yet God called him to deliver His people from Egypt and lead them into the Promised Land. Queen Esther did not want to go to the king to plead for the lives of her people. Yet even though she felt inadequate, she went boldly in obedience and saved the entire nation of Israel from slaughter.

The examples go on and on throughout the Bible. God knows your weaknesses and your imperfections, yet His plan is bigger than anything you can possibly comprehend. He washes away the sins you committed before you knew Him, and He forgives the sins you commit after coming to know Him. God's grace is certainly sufficient to cover all your mistakes—past and future.

Winston Churchill once said, "Success is going from failure to failure without a loss of enthusiasm." Everyone understands failure. If you're not failing, you're not attempting anything very hard. What people want to know is: Do you keep coming back? Is your faith there for you even when you blow it? Is it truly part of your life, or is it just a passing phase like last year's trendy diet? What people are looking for is something that will be there for them even if *they* fail.

So if you've blown it, don't freak out. Don't let it sideline you. Stay in the game and take part in the great commission. Cultivate the attitude that speaker Tim Timmons is talking about when he says, "I'd rather be a flawed diamond than a perfect brick!"

It's Not Up to You

Unsaved people want us to be honest and vulnerable. If we are, Jesus will shine through us. We love what Paul said after the Lord told him, "My grace is sufficient for you":

31

> *So now I am glad to boast about my weaknesses, so*
> *that the power of Christ may work through me.*
> *Since I know it is all for Christ's good, I am quite content with*
> *my weaknesses and with insults, hardships, persecutions, and*
> *calamities. For when I am weak, then I am strong.*
>
> 2 CORINTHIANS 12: 9–10

There will always be a hundred good excuses you could give for not opening your mouth about Jesus. But aren't excuses just smoke-screens we put up to disguise our real reasons for doing or not doing something?

Don't worry about your perceived inadequacies. At times, even the three of us fear we are not competent to effectively represent the Lord. But we push through it for the greater purpose of Christ. Focus on seeking Jesus through all the seasons of your life. As you keep your eyes on Him, you will feel confident in your weaknesses because you trust that His power will come through. Remember, this isn't about you. It's about God and a person who needs Him. Revel in the knowledge that when you are weak, Christ makes you strong.

So how can you talk about Jesus without freaking out? The best way to lower your blood pressure when trying to tell someone that he needs Jesus is to remember that the results are not up to you.

---

1. Throughout this book, whenever we use male pronouns for people (he, his, him) we mean to include both males and females. Writing "he or she saw his or her friend at his or her desk" becomes distracting.

2. Dr. Bill Bright, *Witnessing without Fear* (San Bernardino, Calif.: Here's Life Publishers, 1987), 67.

3. Max Lucado, Stillwater Gifts Daily Calendar (Wheaton, Ill.: Tyndale House Publishers, Inc., 1998).

CHAPTER TWO

F.E.A.R.

Don't be afraid, for I am with you.
Do not be dismayed, for I am your God.
I will strengthen you. I will help you.
ISAIAH 41:10

Jim Says: As soon as I had been hired on as the composer for a new network TV series, I was immediately pushed out of my comfort zone. For the second episode, the producers wanted me to write music to reflect the feeling of the desperate lives of young gang members in New Orleans. The show closed with the final voiceover saying, "We don't know what the answer is to gang killings, and we probably never will." It was a depressing message of hopelessness to millions of viewers across the world.

I knew we had to offer hope, so I came up with a way to change the meaning of the message through my choice of music. I didn't know if the Jewish producers would go for it, but I decided to take the chance.

Now the hopeless voiceover was followed by the sound of a gospel singer singing the hymn "Softly and Tenderly." As an image of a murdered child appeared, the viewer heard, "Jesus is calling for you and for me to come home." And when the final image of a teenage murderer came on the screen, the singer was singing, "Calling, oh sinner, come home."

I thought it was powerful. It gave hope and lifted up the name of Jesus. I was excited...then I freaked out.

What in the world was Steven, the Jewish executive producer, going to say?

I turned in the show to him late Thursday. At 9 A.M. Friday the phone rang. "Jim?" It was Steven.

I swallowed hard, thinking that this was my second and last episode on this series. But Steven said, "I just saw your show and it's *#$@&%^$ incredible! I don't know what it is, but it's the best show we've ever done!"

I thanked him and hung up, smiling. I knew exactly what "it" was!

2

Aaaaaaaagggggghhhhhh

We all feel some trepidation when it comes to sharing our faith. "But I'm afraid I'll freak people out if I tell them about Jesus!" we say. We fear we'll offend the people we witness to. We fear they will think we are fanatics. We fear they will reject us. And, as we discussed in the previous chapter, we fear our own inadequacies and we fear we'll fail.

We are such wimps! We don't know how good we have it in twenty-first-century America. Look at what the early Christians went through. They were literally fed to the lions for proclaiming their faith, and usually the worst thing that happens to us is that someone tells us to be quiet. Even today, Christians around the world are being martyred. At worst we may lose our jobs.

God tells us over and over to fear Him, not people (Psalm 27:1; Proverbs 29:25; Luke 12:4–5). If there ever was anyone who should have been filled with fear, it was King David. His enemies were out to kill him! And yet we see throughout the Psalms that his trust was in the Lord. "I will not fear the tens of thousands drawn up against me on every side," he said (Psalm 3:6, NIV). Thinking about David and the enemies he chose not to fear will put your own fear into perspective—especially the fear of sharing your love for the Lord.

The only one you should fear is the Lord Himself, never other people or your own inadequacies. Theologian Dietrich Bonhoeffer once asked:

> Why should we be afraid of one another, since both of us have only God to fear? Why should we think that our brother would not understand us, when we understood very well what was meant when somebody spoke God's comfort or God's admonition to us, perhaps in words that were halting and unskilled?[1]

David's strength was in the Lord. His strong and clear understanding of who God is conquered his fear and overpowered his insecurities. As you begin to understand what it means to be a witness and what you need to communicate the gospel, you too will gain the confidence you need to overcome your fears.

False Evidence Appearing Real

Most of our fears are unfounded. We have discovered that when we speak about Jesus, people do not usually react to us the way we feared they would. Sometimes we can be like children, afraid of monsters under our beds. When we muster the courage to get down there with a flashlight, we see that it was only shadows that had us spooked.

We like to talk about the fear of witnessing by using the acronym F.E.A.R. It stands for False Evidence Appearing Real. Our fears come from a barrage of false evidence that clouds our minds and eventually begins to seem real to us.

Fear comes straight from the devil. He knows that if we are scared enough, we will not say a word about Jesus Christ. He plays on our insecurities. We all hear his monologue of lies in our heads. It tells us what the other person is "surely" thinking about us and what we're saying. Satan is so good at his lies that his false evidence can appear real. But it is not!

Fear has no basis in truth. If we could get over our fear of talking about the most important topic there is, our whole world would be a different place—or Jesus would have come back by now. One of the reasons it has taken so long to reach the entire planet is because of *fear*. The enemy is prolonging the fight—and he's doing a good job at it.

The Lord knows our struggles, and He can do His mighty work through us despite our fear. He just wants us to be willing to step out in faith. His words are as true for us today as they were for the ancient Israelites:

"This is what the Lord says:
Do not be afraid! Don't be discouraged by this mighty army, for
the battle is not yours, but God's.... You will not even need to fight.
Take your positions; then stand still and watch the Lord's victory.
He is with you, O people of Judah and Jerusalem.
Do not be afraid or discouraged.
Go out there tomorrow, for the Lord is with you!"
2 CHRONICLES 20:15, 17

Go out and face the world each day. Do not be afraid or discouraged. The battle of witnessing is not yours, but God's. You just have to stand firm in your faith and see the deliverance the Lord will give you.

Franklin D. Roosevelt stated the problem succinctly: "The only thing we have to fear is fear itself." Although this is a lesson we cannot teach you, we can give you the most powerful antidote to it. It's the name of Jesus.

The J-Bomb

Have you ever wondered why Jesus is the only name used as a swear word? How many people use the name of Buddha or Mohammed as a curse? There's true, immeasurable power in only one name. Ever notice that anybody, even Christians, can talk about God as being a higher power, our Creator, even our Father—but that we all tend to avoid referring to Him as Jesus Christ?

There's just something powerful about the name of Jesus. Even unbelievers realize it. When you say it, walls start falling down, people's hearts begin to soften (or pound!), and lives start to change. Even when a person seems outwardly hostile and negative, when Jesus' name enters the conversation, something begins churning on the inside.

Dr. Larry Poland, founder of MasterMedia International, says that this happens "because the power of His name is like nuclear fission."[2] Poland says that when we tell Jesus' story to others, we are pouring out energy so powerful that the listener may not be able to handle it. He may get scared and throw it back, run, or get angry. More often, he is dying for something more powerful than himself to run his life and is intrigued by the power contained in the name Jesus Christ. He may ponder it, or even grab for it. But just confronting that kind of power is scary and intimidating.

fis·sion (fish'en) *noun*

A nuclear reaction in which an atomic nucleus, especially a heavy nucleus such as an isotope of uranium, splits into fragments, usually two fragments of comparable mass, with the evolution of from 100 million to several hundred million electron volts of energy.

The name of Jesus is like the power of a nuclear reaction. Once the power is unleashed, you're just there to observe the effect. It's the other person who has to handle the explosion of truth that's been unleashed. He may get scared and try to run away or deflect it. But there's no denying its power.

You can be sure that Satan understands the power of Jesus' name. That's why he doesn't want you using it—except, of course, in vain. He knows that it's the only name under the sun that reaches so deep and evokes such emotional response. So he tries his hardest to keep you from speaking it and others from wanting to hear it. But hey, isn't frustrating the devil's efforts all the more reason to talk about Jesus?

Some people freak out because they know they are engaging in spiritual warfare. War is scary, but it's part of the package of being a Christian. When we speak to an unbeliever about Jesus Christ, we are invading enemy territory and attempting to seize his possessions.

Don't think that just because you can't see the devil, he's not actively opposing you. The hesitation you feel when you want to talk to someone about Jesus is not all from your own lack of confidence. Some of it—maybe most of it—is from Satan himself, fighting back against the power of the name of Jesus.

Just remember that the devil has already lost (Hebrews 10:12–13). Here and now his attacks still feel pretty potent, but the reality is it's only the last, desperate assaults of a defeated enemy.

So cut yourself some slack. Realize that when you are speaking truth, you are taking part in something much larger than yourself. God does not expect you to be some kind of superorator or mega-theologian. All He wants is a willing volunteer. Your job is just to go ahead and speak the name of Jesus and say the words He brings to your mind (Matthew 10:19–20).

Victorya Says: I got a call one day from a stranger named Becky. She was a drug-addicted musician who was an acquaintance of a friend of mine. Becky had just watched Dan, one of her dear friends, die a slow, painful death.

Dan, only forty-three, hadn't accomplished much in his life. He had barely held on to jobs, had kept only a few friends, and had been alienated from his family for years. On his deathbed, Dan had made one request: that a Christian minister conduct his funeral.

Less than thrilled, Becky nonetheless honored his request. She recalled that a fellow musician had a friend who was a minister, and she tracked me down. Angrily, Becky made it clear to me that she was very bitter toward Christians and demanded that I not preach about sin and judgment. She just wanted to honor Dan's request with a pleasant memorial.

I told God I did not want to do it. I guess you could call it fear. I knew I wouldn't know anyone there. I feared the hostile audience I would face and that they would throw me out for mentioning Jesus. And I feared going onto the battlefield alone.

So was I going to do this funeral or not? I told myself I wouldn't do it because I never performed weddings or funerals if I couldn't talk about Jesus. I was not going to walk into a hostile environment just to do a feel-good service with no eternal value.

I called Karen for prayer and guidance. Then I telephoned Becky and told her that as a minister I needed to be free to share whatever I felt God wanted me to share with the mourners. By her reaction, it seemed I was off the hook. But three days later, she called to give me directions to the funeral—for the next day!

I had to research Dan's life and prepare my service overnight. In doing so I discovered that Dan had attended church during his childhood, but had walked away from God in his teens. Then two weeks before his death, he had accepted Jesus as his personal Savior. At the end he read his Bible constantly and told his friends that he hoped they would also make a decision to serve Jesus before it was too late.

Wow! Were those mourners in for a surprise! I went along with my prayer warrior friend Jaki. While Jaki prayed, I told the mourners about the forgiving love of Jesus. Through the dying prayer of a seemingly worthless man, thirty people who would never have darkened the door of a church heard about the one true God. After the service, one of Dan's nurses came up to Jaki and prayed to receive Christ.

There's more! When Becky asked what fee I required, I impulsively said, "If you will read the Bible I hold in my hands, that will be payment enough." She took the Bible and said, "If I say I'm going to do something, I am definitely going to do it. And I have wanted to read this book. The service was everything I dreamed it would be."

I was stunned. The woman I had feared—who five days before had angrily informed me that I was not permitted to share the gospel—had been touched and had vowed to read the Bible. None of my fears had come to pass. They had all turned out to be False Evidence Appearing Real.

2

Get Out of Your Comfort Zone

If you get nothing else out of this book, please hold tightly to this: From this moment on you must not let fear make you a mediocre

Christian. Take risks, stretch, grow, learn, and force yourself to get out of your Christian bubble—your spiritual comfort zone! You never know what God has in store for you when you are willing to be His vessel.

The devil has created an illusion to prevent you from reaching the souls he hopes to take down with him. The illusion is like a filter, subtly altering everything you see through it. Through it everyone appears hostile or cold. But when you remove the filter, you see the same people as they really are—desperately hungry for the bread of life. Defy the devil. Destroy the filter that distorts your perception and makes you afraid to take risks. Most people aren't as opposed to the gospel as he would have you believe.

If you are to step out in faith, you have to be willing to be uncomfortable. People who succeed at anything take risks. Those who are successful in the business world take financial risks. Great Olympic champions push beyond their physical limits and break world records. Christians who stretch their faith muscles catch a glimpse of heaven.

Anyone can be a witness. Just make these actions a part of your life and watch yourself be transformed into an ambassador for the Lord, the likes of which will surprise even you:

- *Believe that the Lord expects to use you.*
- *Pray for the Lord to make you bold.*
- *Learn the tools needed to share your faith. (We'll help you with that in Part II.)*
- *Begin praying for all of the unbelievers in your life.*
- *Step out of your comfort zone and go for it.*

If you consistently apply these five principles to your life, you will never be the same again. You will never be mediocre! And you won't be afraid.

Jim Says: A friend of ours, Rick, was attending a graduate psychology seminar. The teacher required each member to get up in front and confess something personal to the class. Rick felt that this was an opportunity to "come out of the closet" and confess to the class that he was a Christian. He knew it had to be done—and yet he kept stewing about how he could best proclaim the name of Jesus.

As he was trying to work up the nerve to make this big announcement, a woman got up and said, "I have to confess that I am a church lady." She explained how God had come to mean so much to her and said that her spiritual journey had brought her to church. Then she pointed her finger right at Rick and said, "And this all started with you."

She told the class how Rick had invited her to a Christmas party a few months earlier. When she left the party, someone gave her a little pamphlet about God. After she read it, she started going to church. The rest was history.

Rick was now officially out of the spiritual closet—and he hadn't even said a word!

Fear Not

We encourage you to believe the truth of God's Word and to pray for deliverance from the evil obstacle of fear. We promise that if you are willing to take a leap of faith and put yourself at risk for God, He will not leave you stranded. He has commanded us to go out and tell the world about Him; He will not then leave us nor forsake us. Don't let fear grip you.

Remember that in witnessing situations it is normal to feel some degree of anxiety or fear. But the fear is almost always a false alarm!

So you don't have to freak out. The more you push through the fear and speak up anyway, the more you'll see how easy it really is to talk about Jesus.

Every time you speak up, you will gain more confidence because you will see how hungry people are for truth. And you'll realize that you survived the encounter without being beaten and bruised. You may have felt uncomfortable, but you weren't battered.

Are you ready to take part in something bigger than you? Are you ready to take your place on the front lines? Ask God to help you become willing to step out into your mission field for Him.

Fear not! He will be there.

1.   Dietrich Bonhoeffer, *Life Together* (San Francisco: HarperSanFrancisco, 1954), 104, 106.

2.   Larry Poland is the founder of MasterMedia International, a Christian ministry for the entertainment industry. He can be contacted at 330 N. Sixth St., Suite #110, Redlands, CA 92374-3312. Phone (909) 335-7353.

CHAPTER THREE

Pre-Christians Everywhere

"My sheep recognize my voice; I know them,
and they follow me. I give them eternal life, and they will never perish.
No one will snatch them away from me."

JOHN 10:27–28

Victorya Says: Sarah is a gospel singer. One evening she was invited to sing at a rock 'n' roll club where some friends were performing. She had a new song she wanted to try out—a ballad about the amazing grace of God—but she wasn't sure it would go over well at the club. Even so, she decided to give it a go.

For some strange reason, during rehearsal the keyboard player just couldn't get the melody, no matter how many times he tried. Sarah smiled and said, "No problem, I'll just sing it a cappella."

The evening quickly got wild. People were drinking, dancing, and getting out of control. One girl in particular was quite drunk. She was an attractive, longhaired blond in a miniskirt, with three guys surrounding her. Sarah looked at her sadly, knowing that something was going to happen to her that night.

It was late in the evening by the time Sarah was called up on stage. She stood before the rowdy audience, closed her eyes, and began to sing. At her first note, the audience became completely silent.

She'd made it through the first verse and was halfway through the chorus when she heard the keyboard begin to play behind her in perfect harmony. She was thrilled that her friend had finally figured out the melody. As she held the last note, the audience burst into applause.

When Sarah turned around to thank her friend, she was amazed to see that it wasn't he at the keyboard. It was the blond girl from the bar, and she had tears streaming down her face.

Sarah sat down and talked to the girl, Lori. It turned out that Lori was a preacher's kid who used to play the piano in church every Sunday. She had run away from God, her family, and her upbringing, thinking she was missing out on "the good life."

Yet God loved this prodigal daughter so much that He reached out to Lori in that wild club, in the midst of her rebellion, and sent Sarah to sing a song to show her the way home.

Pre-Christians Everywhere

You never know who is teetering on the edge of a decision for Christ. We have seen corrupt, hardened, and angry people—people we would never expect to be open to the gospel—come to Jesus. And sometimes all it takes is a word, a crack in the door, or the slightest invitation. Remember, people are wrestling with *God*, and He's powerful and unrelenting. Sometimes a simple word on your part might be the thing God uses to finally reach someone.

Don't allow yourself to think of anyone as hopeless or beyond God's reach. We can't know who will and who won't ultimately say yes to Jesus. But we do know that it is God's will that everyone come to know Him (1 Timothy 2:4). So we always begin in the belief that all unbelievers in our lives eventually will say yes to Christ, even if they resist right now. No one is hopeless. That's why we think of the unbelievers around us as *pre-Christians*.

We have entered their lives during the pregame show—life without Christ—and we have the privilege of leading them toward the spectacular main event—life with Christ. It's not our place to decide who is worth trying to save and who's hopeless. God is going to surprise us time and time again.

If anyone was hopeless it was Saul of Tarsus. His personal mission in life was to murder Jewish Christians. Yet God had a different plan for him. Despite the fact that Saul was murdering His own, Jesus came down, met him on the road to Damascus, and turned his life around 180 degrees. Saul, renamed Paul, turned out to be one of the most effective witnesses of all time. Did you notice that it was Jesus Himself who told Saul the truth about the gospel? Since there was not one human being who considered Saul a candidate for conversion, it had to be Jesus. We make that same mistake today by not looking at even the most resistant people around us as dynamic believers-to-be.

If God can turn a murdering Christian-hater into a passionate Christian missionary, He can do anything! He can reach that thief, that adulterer, that addict, and even that child molester. Look at all the people around you as special, unique creations of our living God. Pray for them, love them, and treat them as pre-Christians.

Sharecropping

When people think about crops, they usually think of the harvest. They imagine the fields swaying with grain or tall with corn. They rarely give any thought to what the farmer had to do to get the soil ready to bear a crop.

Just as there are different stages in readying crops, there are three main phases in preparing a human heart to receive Christ: cultivating the soil, planting and fertilizing the seed, and harvesting.

> *You know the saying, "One person plants and someone else harvests."*
> *And it's true. I sent you to harvest where you didn't plant; others had*
> *already done the work, and you will gather the harvest.*
>
> JOHN 4:37–38

Each phase is vital in helping a person move toward the Lord. Though all of us might like to be the harvester, the one who leads a person to pray to receive Christ, we have to understand the process and be willing to be used in the other phases as well. Paul said:

> *Each of us did the work the Lord gave us.*
> *My job was to plant the seed in your hearts, and Apollos watered it,*
> *but it was God, not we, who made it grow.... The one who plants and*
> *the one who waters work as a team with the same purpose.*
>
> 1 CORINTHIANS 3:5B–6, 8A

The Lord will use you in all of these stages in different people's lives at different times, and you may not even know it. When you are obedient where you are, standing for Christ even in small ways, you accomplish God's purposes. Won't it be thrilling to get to heaven and discover all the people who came to God because of a seed you sowed when you didn't even know you were sowing?

Let's look a little more closely at the three stages of leading a person to Jesus.

Phase 1: Cultivating a Relationship

The first stage is when we seek to gain the right to tell someone about our Lord by cultivating a relationship with him. It doesn't usually work to just walk up to people and tell them they're going to hell without Jesus.

If you want to tell people about the most important decision they'll ever make—and if you want them to listen when you tell them—you have to earn the right to be heard. Don't lose sight of the truth that we're all recovering humans. You have to gain respect, learn about someone's needs and hurts, and lay a foundation of trust before you tell him that his way will ultimately end in disaster.

You have to cultivate a relationship with nonbelievers, just as Christ cultivates a relationship with you. You do this by letting them know who you are, asking them a lot of questions, and being an attentive listener. You build a friendship or simply find common ground. This is the stage that takes the most time, the most patience, and the most love. Yet it yields the least obvious results for a Christian who longs to see the harvest. If you do this well, when the time comes, you will have permission to speak about Jesus, and you will see a rich harvest.

Here are our top ten tips on how to cultivate a relationship with a non-Christian friend, coworker, classmate, or neighbor:

Top Ten Tips

1. Cultivate your relationship with God first and always.
2. Pray for responsive people to come into your life.
3. Build a reservoir of shared experiences and common interests.
4. Look for opportunities to serve.
5. Look for opportunities to plant "spiritual seeds."
6. Have a "harvest" mentality and be ready to share.
7. Include them in your holidays and special seasons.
8. Eliminate Christianese (more on that later).
9. Be patient! It's a low-pressure, long-range process.
10. Expect results.

Success IN Witnessing

DEFINITION:
Taking the initiative to share Christ in the power of the Holy Spirit
and leaving the results to God.
OR
Taking the initiative to help a person move one step in the process—
not necessarily making "a close."

Because witnessing is a process—it takes time.

the Wrong "Try-Angle"

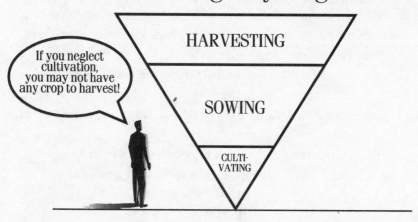

HARVESTING

SOWING

CULTI-
VATING

If you neglect
cultivation,
you may not have
any crop to harvest!

the Right "Try-Angle"

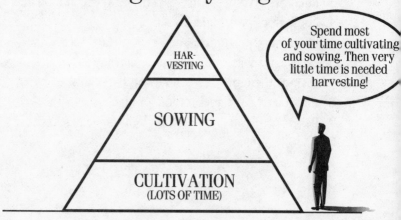

HAR-
VESTING

SOWING

CULTIVATION
(LOTS OF TIME)

Spend most
of your time cultivating
and sowing. Then very
little time is needed
harvesting!

Phase 2: Sowing Seeds

In the second stage you plant seeds of spiritual truth. In this phase you sow the gospel in the pre-Christian's heart, fertilize with examples and new information, and keep weeds in check by rooting out misunderstanding. You sow seeds by being open, asking questions, inviting them to church, and continuing to be a good listener. Sowing seeds takes patience and a willingness to hang in there for the long haul. It may be a slow and gentle process over a long period of time, or it may mean laying out the entire gospel all at once. Just because you get the opportunity to tell the whole plan of salvation doesn't mean the person you're talking with will accept it. Imagine it sinking down into the soil where it may need years to germinate. But don't despair—this is all part of God's plan. The seed grows by itself (Mark 4:26–29).

You never know where someone is in his spiritual journey when you come on the scene. Perhaps you'll be the first to share the Good News; perhaps you'll be the hundredth. Sometimes God allows you to be the one who plants, sometimes the one who fertilizes, sometimes the one who reaps.

Sometimes, as with Paul and Apollos, one person will begin the process and someone else will continue it. Still another person might have the privilege of leading the person to the Lord. This isn't a competition. We don't get more points for more souls. We get points for obeying God. When someone comes to Christ, the whole team scores.

Phase 3: Harvesting the Fruit

The third stage is when you challenge the person to make a decision. This is the most exciting step—and the scariest. It entails making sure a person understands what it means to make a personal commitment to Jesus and then either leading him in prayer or telling him how he can pray to become a Christian. This is the stage that takes the least time, yet yields the greatest rewards to the witnessing Christian. If you have had the privilege of leading someone to the Lord, you know that God has powerfully used you in the new believer's life.

But don't lose focus. It is still just one step in the process, and you won't get a better zip code in heaven for your part in it. You are one of many faithful workers who will all share the joy over this one decision for eternity (John 4:36).

In Part II we will talk about how to actually lead someone through the steps that lead to conversion. Our purpose here is simply to show you where that fits in the whole process.

Karen Says: Soozie was a member of a college ministry staff that was handing out gospel booklets to students on campus. One day she stopped a young man and asked if she could talk to him about the tract. When she showed it to him, he said, "Sure" and listened eagerly. They read through the entire book, and when it came to the page with the prayer of salvation, Soozie said, "Does this represent the desire of your heart?"

The young man said, "Yes."

"Would you like to pray that prayer right now?"

"Yes, but I have to tell you something first. You are the sixth person who has come up to me with this book. When the first person asked me, I wouldn't even let him open the book. I told him I wasn't interested. I allowed the second person to get to the first page. The third person I let get a little farther. After I sent away the fifth person, I knew I wanted to hear more. They were all so kind and polite, even when I cut them off or sent them away. Last night I prayed that God would send me one more person so I could hear the whole message. So, yes, now I'm ready to pray that prayer."

3

Crop Dusting

Be warned: As soon as you identify yourself with Christ, whether you realize it or not, you become an official crop duster.

Your job is always the same: to move a person one step closer to Jesus. That's something else that should lower your blood pressure about witnessing. You don't have to move them the whole way, just one tiny step. You never know if the person you're talking to is twenty steps or one step from coming to Christ. Be willing to be used in any way you can. Don't get discouraged if you are often the cultivator or the seed sower. You can get frustrated if a powerful conversation did not seem to have moved the person any closer to accepting Jesus. You can leave thinking, "What is my problem?" or "I really blew it" or worse, "Well, I'll never do that again!"

If the devil can't keep you from talking to a person the first time, the best he can hope to do is prevent it from happening again. He knows how God's overall plan works—and he knows that you usually don't. So he'll tell you that if the person didn't get on his knees right then and there that you're a total washout in the witnessing department. "Sit down before you hurt yourself or somebody else," he whispers. "Leave this to the professionals."

Don't let the lack of visible results affect your understanding of the experience. You may not feel like you're making a spiritual impact on someone if all you're doing is cultivating a friendship. But if that person has never had a Christian friend, you could be having a powerful effect on him. If you prayed, God used you, even if you didn't "make a close." You could have moved that person one step closer to Jesus—a step that will make an eternal difference. You don't know all that God has planned in that person's life. You just have to be faithful and prepared. You may never know the full impact you had on a person's life until you get to heaven.

Jim and Karen Say: We have a friend, Lynette, who has a burning desire to lead others to Jesus. She takes advantage of every opportunity, and yet her efforts always seem to fall on deaf ears. She began grieving over this, certain she was not making an impact. We pointed out to her that she is raising two boys who love Jesus and who are quite bold in their faith. In fact, her four-year-old has already introduced the little neighbor girl to the Lord. We told her that by raising her boys in the Lord, she was actually leading others to Jesus. She was encouraged to know that the Lord was giving her the desires of her heart—just not in the way she had expected.

3

Two Missionary Fields

Now that you understand the way a pre-Christian moves through the phases of God's harvest plan, let's talk about the two main fields you will find yourself tending. Pre-Christians fall into two groups, and Christians should always be witnessing to both:

- *People you know (family, friends, neighbors, classmates, coworkers)*
- *People you don't know (friends of friends, total strangers)*

Sounds obvious, right?

Whether you're talking with friends or strangers, you can know that the process is the same. You tell them about Jesus by the power of the Holy Spirit and then leave the results to God. You may be the person who gets to harvest the crop, or you may not. If you do get the opportunity to challenge someone to make a decision about Jesus, it's a great thing. If you don't, it's still wonderful to be a part of the process.

Though it may seem odd, it's often actually easier to talk to strangers about Jesus than it is to talk about Him to family and friends. Let's consider strangers first. All Christians need to be ready and willing to be effective witnesses in the lives of strangers who cross their paths.

Strangers in the Night

Talking to strangers about Jesus is often easier because you have nothing to lose. When no cherished relationship is at risk, you can talk more openly. In addition, conversations with strangers are usually brief, and since you'll probably never see the person again, you feel you have to get to the point quickly and boldly go for it.

You may be next to someone waiting in line for a movie when you feel God prompting you to say something. You have about a three-minute wait. How do you build rapport, earn the right to be heard, and share the gospel in three minutes? You can't! So what do you do? Forget about it? No! Believe that God has orchestrated this appointment and boldly take advantage of it by starting a conversation about Jesus.

In short-term encounters, you don't have time to go through the three phases of harvest. So how can you earn the right to talk to them about eternal matters if you'll only talk with them for a few minutes on a plane? This person most likely won't come to Easter church service with you or spend time with you to see how your faith works on a daily basis.

In a conversation with a fellow air passenger, you may only have the chance to plant a few seeds or maybe water some that are already there. But you never know. If you are the sixth person to talk to him about Jesus in a month, you may find yourself getting to harvest another worker's crop. And should the plane ride get a little bumpy, it's amazing how quickly you might get the chance to share the heart of the gospel.

When you find yourself in a potential witnessing situation with a stranger, pray for God's leading, introduce yourself, and always ask his name. Try to bring up the Lord in any way that is appropriate to that situation. You can give your testimony, telling him how Jesus has met some need in your life. You can ask him questions to find out his specific need or struggle. You can even pray for him right there. Whatever you do, be bold and willing to be used by God. Then the opportunities will surely come.

"But how do I even get into a spiritual conversation when talking to a stranger?" you may be asking. It can be so frustrating to be in a conversation with a stranger and not know how to turn it into a discussion of spiritual things. That's where transitions are helpful.

All it takes is a change of mindset to think creatively of ways to have meaningful discussions with others. There are all kinds of transitions possible in everyday conversations. A good way to move into a spiritual dialogue is to consider what Jesus would say. He didn't preach as much as He asked questions and gave analogies. And He was the master of transitions.

Your goal is to be able to transition smoothly in and out of any topic by merely asking a question or offering another perspective on the topic at hand. Over the years, Jim has earned the title of "king of transitions." Here are some of his examples:

- **Social-issues transitions:** "The American family is in such a crisis today with more and more families splitting apart. Divorce is rampant. What do you think is going to save them? I know that for me personally, if I didn't believe in God I would be scared to death to get married."

- **Scientific transitions:** "Scientists keep talking about the Big Bang, and they say that time and space actually have a beginning. Have you heard this? Do you think this is all a big cosmic accident or is there some designer behind it all?"

- **Geographic transitions:** "Have you ever been to Pasadena? We go to church there. Have you ever heard of Lake Avenue Church? We call it the Worship Emporium because it's a huge structure on the 210 freeway."

- **Fashion transitions:** "I love the cross you're wearing. Does that have some meaning to you or is it just a cool piece of jewelry? My husband gave me my cross...." or "What does that say on your shirt? Do you really believe what that says?"

- **Book transitions:** "What's that book you're reading? Do you like to read? Have you ever read the Bible? Did you know that the Bible has been the number one bestseller in America for so long that it's not even listed anymore?"

- **Political transitions:** "Do you really think that a Democrat or a Republican can influence the moral status of our country? To me it comes down to a moral issue. It seems that people just have to be willing to choose to do the right thing, regardless of which party is in charge. What do you think?"

- **Relationship transitions:** "As a parent I'm now beginning to understand the free will God gave us. For instance, I can tell my four-year-old to play in the front yard, but to not go off the grass. He has the choice to do what I say or to run out into the street and get hit by a car. I can't make him stay there, but I can explain to him the consequences and then let him make his own choice based on his free will. I see God giving us free will with the same freedom to choose, but also with consequences. Does that make sense?"

When your encounter with a stranger is finished, pray for that person and ask the Lord to water the seed you have planted. Congratulations! The Lord has just used you! You could have just made an eternal difference in someone's life. Now that's a thrilling high!

Jim Says: Karen and I were talking to an acquaintance who was visiting us. It soon became apparent that he had no spiritual foundation and no purpose in life. He worked a nine-to-five job and partied his money away on the weekends. His one prized possession in life was his shot-glass collection. We longed for him to know Jesus, yet it seemed we were getting nowhere in offering him some hope and purpose for his life. Finally I just took the leap and transitioned into his favorite topic.

"George, how is your shot-glass collection going?" I asked. "Do you have a shot glass from Boise, Idaho? You do? You know, I have a friend who moved up there to start a new church. Have you ever heard of Boise Community Church?"

There it was. We were talking about church. From then on the conversation focused on the Lord.

3

Friends and Family

There is an inverse relationship between how well you know someone and how much time you take laying out your faith in God. With people you know, you typically have more time to cultivate relationships and to demonstrate more fully who Jesus is to you. The downside, of course, is that you may actually risk your relationship with these people by bringing in the nuclear fission-powered name of Jesus. Also, unbelievers are often more defensive when talking about something as personal as this with someone they know well.

It may help to realize that you aren't the only person in the situation afraid to talk about Jesus. The person you're talking to may be afraid of it, too. It's the supreme question, the ultimate issue. People go to great lengths to avoid talking about things of eternal importance. Sometimes it helps us get past our own fears to realize that our family member or friend is just as scared as we are. Usually they are more so. They often see you as the knowledgeable one and themselves as the less-informed party. Just understanding this dynamic may help you relax. You are standing firm for God, proclaiming the most powerful name in existence. What can they bring to bear against that? Be encouraged!

Effectively communicating the truth about Jesus to family members and friends requires compassion, love, and especially patience. That's why telling the whole story takes time—weeks, months, and even years. We have been praying for decades for some of our family members to embrace the Lord!

No matter who it is, you will be more effective when you have earned the person's respect. You earn that respect by living a consistent life of integrity, following solid biblical standards, and being a good worker or a faithful friend.

Even when respect is there, there will be times when pre-Christian friends and family members may snub your efforts to share your faith. Don't be discouraged. Remember that Jesus Himself was not accepted in His own hometown (Luke 4:24). If they rebuff you when you reach out in Jesus' name, they may not really be rejecting you, but the Lord you represent (1 Thessalonians

4:8). Be patient and loving with those pre-Christians you know: Take it slowly, pray, and don't push.

There are some things you can do to have an eternal impact on someone you love, even if your words seem to be falling flat. If you pray for someone's salvation, you have not failed. Indeed, we are convinced that no one is saved without someone having prayed for him. If you are committed to becoming more Christlike every day and are motivated by genuine love and compassion for others, you cannot fail, even if your friends don't ever accept Jesus. You succeed in witnessing—no matter the visible effects—when you obey God's command to share His love in the power of the Holy Spirit. But do it with gentleness and respect. That's what our dear pastor friend Jeff calls being a "mighty warrior attack sheep"!

Karen Says: In June of my freshman year at USC, less than one month after I became a Christian, I went home to spend the summer with my mom and dad. I was shocked to see that my parents' marriage was falling apart. I was devastated. It broke my heart to see how angry and upset my mom was. After being home about a week, I found myself telling Mom that I had become a Christian.

She was immediately interested. She wanted what I had found. Right there on our back patio, my mom prayed to accept Jesus as her Lord and Savior. It was so natural and so exciting—maybe because I had no idea what I was doing!

Right after we prayed, Mom said that we should tell my grandmother about Jesus. Two weeks later, the three of us had lunch, and I told my grandma the same story about how we had both become Christians. It made sense to her, too, and she also prayed to accept Jesus.

My grandma is now in heaven and my parents' marriage is better than it's ever been in almost fifty years. And I am still amazed at how God gave me favor in my own home.

Lifestyles of the Rich and Famous

There are two groups of pre-Christians who are often overlooked when we think about who needs Jesus. The first are people we call celebrities. They are the rich and the famous.

Even though the world thinks they have it all together, celebrities—movie stars, pro athletes, politicians, or powerful executives—make up perhaps one of the most spiritually bankrupt segments of our population. Spirituality may be currently in vogue among celebrities, but it has never been cool to be sold out to Jesus Christ.

You might expect that even without a relationship with God, wealthy and powerful people would be happy and fulfilled because they appear to lack nothing. But as Blaise Pascal once said, there is a God-shaped vacuum in the heart of each man that can be filled only by God the Creator, made known through Jesus Christ.

Trust us, even the rich and famous need Jesus. People without a personal relationship with God are, by definition, not satisfied. Nowhere is that more evident than in Hollywood, where people try frantically to achieve or desperately to maintain an incredible standard of living or fame. Marilyn Monroe defined our business best when she said,

---

"They'll pay you fifty-thousand dollars for a kiss and fifty cents for your soul."

We want to tell them that Jesus said:

> *"What good will it be for a man if he gains*
> *the whole world, yet forfeits his soul?"*
> MATTHEW 16:26, NIV

We know many people in Hollywood who have it made in the eyes of the world. Their shelves are covered with Academy Awards, Emmy Awards, Gold Records, and other accolades. And yet they are restless and dissatisfied. Life apart from God is empty, perhaps especially so for celebrities. There are many shows on television that profile the rich and famous. They are filled with tragic stories of people who had everything—eveything except God—but whose disillusionment led them into drugs, alcohol, despair, and ultimately death.

The Bible says: "There is a way that seems right to a man, but the end is death" (Proverbs 16:25, NIV). Actor Phil Hartman's wife killed him in a murder/suicide. Police blamed his wife's drug and alcohol addiction and her obsessive jealousy. Actor-comedian Chris Farley died of a drug overdose just as his idol, John Belushi, did. Princess Diana's shocking death touched the world. And the real story of Marilyn Monroe's death may never be known.

The rich and famous are really no different than members of any other social group. They just exemplify one of the extremes of the human condition. It's crystal clear to us after all these years in the media is that money and fame simply cannot satisfy the soul. We've discovered something else surprising: It is far easier for the unbeliever to feel hope for the future *before* great success than for the rich and famous to hold onto hope *after* success. Many can handle unhappiness before success because they hope that once they hit it big, life will be wonderful. But what happens when they achieve everything they hoped for?

We see it time after time in the entertainment industry. The up-and-coming star is the hottest name in Hollywood. He has the world at his fingertips. Then something happens. He's arrived, but now that he has, there's nothing here. *Is that all there is?* he asks himself. He's like the hero of *Citizen Kane:* Nothing is denied him, yet he is terribly empty. He begins striving to find meaning in what he thought was all he ever needed. When he doesn't find it, his despair can be overwhelming.

Madonna Says: All my will has always been to conquer some horrible feeling of inadequacy. I'm always struggling with that fear. I push past one spell of it 'and discover myself as a special human being, and then I get to another stage and think I'm mediocre and uninteresting. And I find a way to get myself out of that. Again and again. My drive in life is from this horrible fear of being mediocre. And that's always pushing me, pushing me. Because even though I've become Somebody, I still have to prove that I'm Somebody. My struggle has never ended, and it probably never will.[1]

3

The reason it's difficult for a wealthy person to find Jesus is not because his money satisfies his needs. It's not that he's filled his God-shaped void with things. That's impossible. It's hard for him to trust God because the more dissatisfied he is, the more obsessed he becomes with trying to find a solution on his own. That's all he knows how to do.

He will work longer and harder and stay busier and busier. When work doesn't satisfy, he may buy more stuff, have an extramarital affair, or abuse alcohol and drugs. He will try anything to dull the pain and fill the void. Ironically, the one place he doesn't look is to Jesus because he doesn't want to appear weak or because he's afraid he'll have to give up the very lifestyle that is making him miserable. People like this become experts at hiding their fears, yet they may be waiting for someone to love them enough to tell them about Jesus.

Anthony Hopkins Says: I'm just very selfish. If somebody doesn't like what I am, I don't hang around trying to win anybody's approval. I may have screwed up a lot of my life, I may have hurt a few people. I'm not a very good husband, I'm not a good father. I'm a roamer. I think I'm a bit of a nihilist, really. The day Jenni [his current wife] met me she knew she was taking on a load of trouble. I've been troubled for years. I don't know quite with what. Something troubles me, and I don't know what it is, but it brings me a lot of restlessness.[2]

Now you understand why we see ourselves as missionaries to a spiritually starving people. We love these people and want them to have so much more than what they have. And we want you to feel the same way about the high-profile people you may work and live with. If you are friends with a well-to-do person who doesn't know Jesus, know that the Lord brought you two together for a divine purpose. Have compassion on him; touch him in prayer; intercede for him that he might not gain the whole world but forfeit his soul. His search will not end happily until he finds a personal relationship with Jesus.

Preaching to the Choir

There's a second segment of the population that is often overlooked by those who would tell lost people about Jesus: church members. If a person is in church with you every Sunday, sings in choir, says amen, and carries a Bible, he is a Christian, right? If that person works for a Christian company or ministry, he is certainly saved, right? You would be surprised. Churches, ministries, and even seminaries attract lost people like magnets. Don't assume.

In some parts of the country a strong church life is a cultural imperative. The majority of the population goes to church on Sunday (or Saturday night) because...well...because that's just how it's done. Particularly in the South and Midwest, restaurants occasionally play Christian music; local newspapers sometimes quote a Scripture or offer a spiritual message for the day; and the front page of the entertainment section might review a Christian concert—even favorably. Jesus appears to be everywhere. But is He really being worshiped?

We say someone's preaching to the choir if he's trying to convince people of something they already believe. It's energy uselessly spent. But the reality of it, especially in places where there is social pressure to go to church, is that there may well be unsaved people in the choir loft.

For the most part people attend church in our country because they want to get closer to God. If they aren't interested in the Lord, they usually don't waste their time there. Some churchgoers, however, attend church out of family habit to feel religious. Many of these people know Christ as only a mythical figure of religion or as a good man.

There are also people who go to church because they are searching for something. Even though they don't know what it is, they think maybe they'll find it at church. According to some estimates, every Christian church in America is supposed to have at least one unbeliever in attendance every Sunday.

65

Don't assume that all of your acquaintances at church are Christians. Find out about their spiritual journeys. Ask questions. If you feel you should, share the plan of salvation with them until you are sure that they have accepted Jesus as their personal Savior.

Begin to listen carefully to everyone's words—whether secular friends or church friends. People often will be very descriptive when discussing their opinions. They may drop their guard and reveal their true beliefs. Ask your Christian friends when they came to know Jesus personally and see what they say. If they *do* have a personal relationship with the Lord, then you'll have a rich time of exchanging personal testimonies. If they don't know Jesus personally, then you have the wonderful pleasure of telling them about the God they are seeking in church each week.

Freak Not

God commands us to tell people about Him. We may think some people are hopeless, but God says He desires for all to be saved. We struggle not to envy those people who have so much more than we do, yet God tells us that none of that ultimately matters. We want to tell others about the Truth, but we can't seem to even change the topic of conversation. These paradoxical truths are hard to understand.

So what do we do?

We pray; we learn how to talk about Jesus; and we pray some more. Soon we'll see that the burden is not ours at all. It belongs to our mighty God, who can speak in paradoxes, ask the impossible of us, and then tell us not to worry about anything. So step out of your spiritual comfort zone and trust the God to whom you've committed your life.

And don't freak out!

1. "Misfit," *Vanity Fair* (April 1991), 98.
2. "Anthony Hopkins," *Showbiz* (16 September 1996).

CHAPTER FOUR

Lights, Camera, Action

"The harvest is so great, but the workers are so few.
So pray to the Lord who is in charge of the harvest;
ask him to send out more workers for his fields."

MATTHEW 9:37–38

Victorya Says: It was done, finally! After five months of living in my new home, I had finally completed my landscaping. Everything was perfect—for a few weeks.

Then it happened. In the midst of my gorgeous yaupon hollys, crepe myrtles, azaleas, and mugo pines, I discovered tiny weeds peeking through. I ignored them at first, but that turned out to be the worst thing I could do. In no time, every weed had grown inches. Oh no, not my new garden! I ran to the store for a bottle of Round-Up.

What I learned was that frequent up-close checkups are crucial in order to maintain a weed-free environment. From far away the garden looks beautiful. It takes a closer look to reveal undesirable growth. If I were to refuse to take that closer look, the weeds would ultimately destroy my garden. Now every few days I walk through my yard looking closely for sprouting weeds. .

4

Get Ready, Get Set...

All right! You've put away the old excuses, gotten past your fears, and taken a good look at the mission field around you. Now you're ready to get down to business, aren't you? Well, let's get to it.

This chapter will tell you everything you need to know before you open your mouth to share the gospel. We'll talk about readying yourself for action, watching for God's leading, and moving people toward Jesus without saying a word.

There are three steps you should take to prepare to talk about Jesus. Because you never know when you're being watched or when you'll be called upon to witness, you need to check that these things are in place before you start each day.

1. Get straight with God.

Aren't our lives very much like our gardens? They have seasonal and daily needs. The seasons are for planting, fertilizing, feeding, and pruning. Equally important is the need for regular weeding. We need to come before God daily in prayer. Just as weeds will take over if we ignore them, our lives will become a tangled mess of unrighteousness if we avoid taking a close look at the condition of our hearts. The larger the weed of our sin, the more it damages our reputation in the eyes of the world.

We encourage you to take a close look at the garden of your heart. It may appear weed-free from a distance, but God has a close-up view. What weeds are sprouting in your life? Is there worry, fear, envy, criticism, jealousy, bitterness, gossip, or pride? If so get out the "Round-Up" (God's Word) and spray those weeds while they are still just sprouts. If we open ourselves up to God daily, the Holy Spirit will reveal the weeds that need to be exterminated.

2. Get a prayer life.

Through the years, we have been overwhelmed by the power of praying for our unbelieving friends. We are now convinced that prayer should be at the beginning, the middle, and the end of every situation, every conversation, every decision, and every action of every day.

If you fast for forty days to seek God's face but don't pray, you're just on a hunger strike. If you share your faith with pre-Christians but don't pray, you're just preaching at them. You're a clanging gong.

Praise Jesus for who He is. Thank Him for what He's done for you. Pray to be right before Him. Confess your sins. Pray for your family, friends, people of influence, neighbors, and your boss. Pray for people you love and those you don't like. Pray for Christians and, of course, for pre-Christians. As we've said, we are convinced that no one is saved without first having had someone, somewhere, praying for him (1 Timothy 2:1–4). Prayer just seems to be the way God includes us in His bigger plan.

Go to your prayer closet (or couch or car) every day. Offer up your requests freely. Open your heart to God's prompting and be willing to do what He says. If you do, you'll discover the truth of a statement by C. S. Lewis: "The purpose of prayer is not to change our circumstances, but to change us."

Karen Says: I became a Christian as a freshman in college. A year later I found out that my childhood piano teacher was a Christian and had been praying for me since I was a little girl.

3. Get an attitude check.

What is the condition of your heart? Talking about Jesus requires great humility. We've seen people who were self-righteous about their spiritual "conquests" and witnessing abilities. Nothing turns pre-Christians off more quickly than holier-than-thou Christians.

Arrogant attitudes have kept many unsaved people from finding out about God. Sharing your faith is not about boasting to others that you're right and they're wrong. It's about realizing how much we all need Jesus. We humbly pass on the Good News of Christ. As we do, we realize that we are merely beggars leading other beggars to bread!

What about your attitude toward unbelievers? We have sometimes seen Christians look down on unbelievers because of their behavior, dress, habits, or past. That's not only silly, it's hypocritical. How can we be mad at a lost person for acting like a lost person? Pre-Christians have come into churches, seeking forgiveness and hope, and have actually been turned away because they didn't look or act or sound like everyone else. Paul reminds us that we were once just like them:

Don't you know that those who do wrong will have no share in the Kingdom of God? Don't fool yourselves. Those who indulge in sexual sin, who are idol worshipers, adulterers, male prostitutes, homosexuals, thieves, greedy people, drunkards, abusers, and swindlers—none of these will have a share in the Kingdom of God.

There was a time when some of you were just like that, but now your sins have been washed away, and you have been set apart for God. You have been made right with God because of what the Lord Jesus Christ and the Spirit of our God have done for you. (1 Corinthians 6:9–11, emphasis added)

Some church members emphasize the first part of Paul's statement, but choose to ignore the second part. The fact that a person is unsaved does not give us the right to disparage him in any way. "On the contrary," said theologian Dietrich Bonhoeffer, "it is to accord him the one real dignity that man has, namely, that though he is a sinner, he can share in God's grace and glory and be God's child."[1]

We are all in need of God's mercy. We were all just as despicable and unclean before Him as others still are. But He accepted us anyway! Enthusiastically pass on to others the baton of love and forgiveness that someone held out to you. But do it humbly.

The WWJD question, popular in the 1990s, is a great self-check: "I wonder, what would Jesus do right now?" That's the attitude you want to have when entering situations in which you want to talk about Jesus. Be gentle, be sensitive, be bold.

Ready for Battle

When a soldier knows a battle is imminent, he gets ready for it. He dons his uniform, straps on his protection, gathers his equipment, and checks his weapons. He makes sure he understands his commander's orders. He gets into position. He probably sees his life flash before his eyes and says a prayer.

By preparing yourself each day to witness for the Lord, you will never have to say that God used you "despite yourself" (2 Timothy 2:15). You will know that God is using you fully because you were equipped and prepared for the task. Face each day on the offense, with your armor on and your confidence in the Lord. Then all He asks you to do is to stand firm and see the deliverance He has for you and for those you care about.

A Tugging on Your Heart

Now that you're ready for action, let's talk about listening for God's directions.

Have you ever had the sudden thought at an off-the-wall time or place that you should bring up Jesus to someone near you? If you are seeking God daily, you will begin to hear Him speak to you through what we call a tugging on your heart. That is the Holy Spirit speaking to you. And He has chosen that moment for a reason. Perhaps someone is praying for that individual at that very instant, and God has chosen you to walk by and talk to him.

The still, small voice of the Holy Spirit is the voice of a gentleman, full of wisdom and truth. You have the choice each time to ignore it or to listen to it. When you listen, you enter the supernatural realm of God's agenda. The Holy Spirit will use you in the most thrilling ways. You will partake in God's resurrection power as He uses you to lovingly nudge the unsaved one step closer to Him.

Unfortunately, if you're like us, sometimes you're going to choose to ignore that gentle tug. Think back on your own life: Have you noticed times when you felt compelled to talk about Jesus with someone, but it was just too much effort? That was a missed opportunity.

Victorya Says: I frequently travel by air, and I find it interesting that sometimes I am prompted to share Christ with my seatmate and other times it doesn't even occur to me.

One time a thirteen-year-old boy was seated in the window seat, I was on the aisle, and there was an empty chair between us. I greeted him when I sat down—and immediately felt God tugging at my heart saying this boy needed to hear about Him.

"Oh no, not now, Lord," I told Him. "I'm too tired, and I'm just not in the mood. It's a long flight. I'll talk to him later." He kept tugging and I kept resisting. Finally I got mad. "God, I am not going to do this! Find someone else this time."

At that instant, I felt a tap on my shoulder. A woman leaned over and asked if the center seat was available. My heart just dropped. God's timing was right and I blew it!

Divine Appointments

"Lemme at 'em!" You've got your gear ready for action, you've got your ears open for God's directions—now all you need is a chance. You need a divine appointment.

Divine appointments are those moments when God puts you in the right place at the right time to share His message with someone. Each day, ask the Lord to help you keep your eyes open for His divine appointments so that you don't miss any opportunities. God has been working on the hearts of the unbelievers who will cross your path. He orchestrates things perfectly so they will have special moments to hear about Him.

Who are His instruments for delivering that message? Christians. You.

Victorya Says: My brother, Dave, got the phone call saying our grandfather had only three months to live. It turned out to be only one week. Though Dave had a job that made it almost impossible for him to leave, he felt God urging him to get on a plane to be with our grandpa. So he took a plane, then drove two hours to the remote hospital where Grandpa lay dying.

When he walked into the hospital lobby, our dad met him and told him that the prognosis was not good. Grandpa had slipped into a coma and most likely would not even know that Dave was in the room.

Just as Dad was giving him the update, the elevator opened and a distraught woman walked out. Dave immediately recognized her as a former customer who had moved to this small town years ago. They greeted each other, and Dave found out that she had just learned that she had a malignant tumor. She was devastated. Dad and Dave asked if they could pray with her right there. With tears running down her face, she accepted.

Dave thought that he was there to be with Grandpa. But God had arranged a divine appointment for him to be there for someone else.

As you start praying for divine appointments, be ready to receive the oddest calls, find yourself in the strangest meetings, and be part of the most surprising conversations. Keep a lookout for people you hardly ever see anymore. It's amazing how just praying to be alert to His gentle touch will cause you to see so much. Keep a special watch for coincidences, because what may seem coincidental may in fact be providential.

Divine appointments often happen at the most inopportune times. But when you've prayed to be used of God, you have to be willing to be available when He calls. Always remember that God knows the bigger picture. He knows the full story of the life of the unsaved person you have encountered, and He knows what that person needs to hear right then.

Ask for a divine appointment and see what wonderful "coincidences" occur.

Jim and Karen Say: The Thursday before Super Bowl weekend last year, Christopher, our eight-year-old, was diagnosed with a brain tumor. It was very large and had to be removed immediately, so we scheduled surgery for Monday morning.

Christopher was admitted to a room with four beds. It quickly became obvious that as severe as our son's condition was, the other three children were much worse. Soon so many of our friends and family began arriving that our little area of the room was constantly brimming with activity, prayer, laughter, and commotion—to the point of bothering the other patients. On Saturday we were moved to a semiprivate room.

That evening there was a knock on our door. It was Sandy, the mother of one of the other struggling babies. She asked if we had a moment to talk privately. She said that she had been watching us from the moment we arrived and that she was amazed at how we were handling the situation—so differently from the other families. She wanted to find out why.

Right there, we got to tell Sandy about Jesus, His promises, His faithfulness to us, and the strength we were getting from Him. Sandy was moved to tears, and we prayed for her. She asked the Lord to take control of her life. Then suddenly she said she had to leave because her husband would be looking for her, and he didn't like her talking about God.

By Sunday evening, we were exhausted. Christopher's favorite aunt offered to stay with him so we could go home to get some sleep before his early morning surgery. We kissed our sleeping wonder boy good night and left. On our way toward the elevator, Sandy came running up to us. She said she had told her husband about our conversation, and now he wanted to talk to us too. If we could just wait for him to finish talking to a doctor, they would like to talk to us now.

After waiting about fifteen minutes, we both started to laugh. There we were, so wanting to go home, yet God had chosen that particular moment—only nine hours before our son's brain surgery—to have us wait for two strangers so we could tell them about Him. It seemed absurd, and yet God's ways are not our ways.

At last we sat down with Sandy and Bob and told them that Jesus was our only real strength. We got to pray for Bob and recommend a church for them to attend. At 10:30 P.M. we walked out of the hospital knowing that angels were rejoicing. It was incredible!

God orchestrated wonderful miracles that weekend, and we're not just talking about Christopher, who is completely back to normal. God had an even bigger plan than just healing Christopher. And all we did was show up.

4

Wordless Witness

Sometimes you can make the loudest statement about Jesus without even opening your mouth. We can get so caught up in our words, worried about saying the right thing and not saying the wrong thing, that we don't allow the Lord to quietly work through us. Most of us don't really believe that the Lord can move in someone else's life without our words.

"Proclaim the gospel at all times; when necessary, use words,"
FRANCIS OF ASSISI

Words alone—even perfectly uttered, theologically orthodox words—do not persuade. If they are not matched by actions, they are without force. On the other hand, if you live out your Christianity in silent sincerity, even a horribly bungled verbal delivery will be persuasive. Isn't that a relief?

Jim Says: Our friend Sally had just become a Christian and was home visiting her family. Her brother hated Sally's new faith and had told her in the past to leave God out of their relationship. This time she decided not to say a word to him about

God, but just to love him. At midday her brother turned to Sally and said very angrily, "Stop talking about Him!" When Sally asked what he was talking about, he replied, "You keep saying Jesus' name, and I told you not to talk to me about Him."

Sally had not said one word about Jesus. Just her presence spoke of the power of God—and her brother couldn't stand it.

Here are three ways to proclaim Jesus without words.

1. Practice random acts of kindness.

What is a random act of kindness? It's doing something kind for someone for no reason and with no strings attached. It's showing God's love in a tangible way. You can show kindness through word or deed, but either way, it must come from the heart.

It is through such acts of kindness that you show God's love to the unbelieving world. C. N. Bovee once said that kindness is a language the dumb can speak and the deaf can understand. Mother Theresa said that kind words might be short and easy to speak, but their echoes are endless.

People don't expect us to give them something for nothing, but Jesus does. We as Christians should love others like Christ loved us (John 13:34). Through these acts of kindness, you become "Jesus with skin on," showing the world that the Spirit of Jesus is alive and active on planet earth. Author Steve Sjogren calls random acts of kindness "servant evangelism":

> Servant evangelism is one method…in a society where other forms of sharing the gospel often meet a great deal of resistance—one which feels it's heard too much "God-talk"

and not seen enough "God-activity"—servant evangelism seems to be a fruitful way for Christians to share God's love with their community.[2]

Sjogren says that the members of his church witness in their neighborhoods by offering something for nothing. They offer free car washes, hand out sodas at Little League games, and give Popsicles to joggers. He says that when people are handed something with no strings attached, they may at first be suspicious. But that act of kindness often prompts them to begin pouring out their life stories to the generous strangers. That's when his church members get the chance to tell the reason behind what they're doing: they want to show God's love in a tangible way.

Victoria Says: David is an actor friend of ours. One day he asked his agent, who is not a Christian, out to lunch. He had no agenda for the meeting. They had a pleasant time just talking. He paid for the meal and then, a few days later, wrote her a note thanking her for a nice lunch and expressing his appreciation to her for being his agent.

The next day she called David practically in tears. She said she had never received a note like that from any of her clients. She said it meant more to her than she could express. David made a lasting impact on his agent—and he never even mentioned God.

We challenge you to make a special effort to start performing random acts of kindness. In this world, everyone seems to have an agenda. "I'll scratch your back if you scratch mine." Is it any wonder that people find it hard to believe that someone would give them something valuable for free? Imagine how it will stand out! Let us be different.

Random acts of kindness cultivate relationships, pull down fences, and will one day give you the right to tell others about the source of your kindness. Brainstorm with your friends and family about how you can reach out to your pre-Christian friends, coworkers, neighbors, and family with random acts of kindness. Make it fun!

Jim Says: I was writing the score for a TV special and found out that one of the producers loved Mrs. Fields' cookies. I wanted to reach out to her, so I brought a bag of warm Mrs. Fields' cookies to one of our meetings. She was shocked. She thought it was the nicest thing in the world. It was so easy on my part, and yet it touched her and made a huge difference in our relationship.

Now the students in our class bring me Mrs. Fields' cookies!

2. Pray.

Prayer is probably the most effective way to touch someone without speaking a word. Because God is the one who changes hearts, He is the one who transforms your prayers into opportunities. You may not always want to tell someone that you're praying for his conversion. It's easy to be misunderstood for things like that. It's okay to just keep it between you and God.

Before you begin praying for that special pre-Christian, consider one thing: If you do, his life might begin to fall apart. As C. S. Lewis once said, "Pain is the megaphone God uses to get the attention of a deaf world." When you pray for the Lord to work in a person's life, it may turn out to be a crisis intervention! God uses whatever means it takes to get his attention. Don't pray for disaster—but don't be surprised by one, either. On the other hand, the person's life might get dramatically better. You never know. But whatever the scenario, faithful prayers will bring change.

When we teach our class, we start the first week by asking each class member to commit to pray for a friend or coworker at least once a day for the entire ten weeks. That person should be someone they know and of the same gender.

Karen Says: Melanie came to the first week of our class and said sheepishly that she had no unsaved friends in town. The whole class committed to pray for Melanie and for the Lord to bring a pre-Christian into her life.

One day a couple of weeks later, Melanie came to class with a postcard that she had just received in the mail. It was from an old friend in New York asking Melanie to get to know the lady whose name, address, and phone number were on the card. She said that this lady, who was not a Christian, was new in L.A. and needed a friend. Melanie couldn't believe this specific answer to prayer.

We want you to commit to pray for pre-Christians. Stop right now, choose a friend or coworker, and commit to pray for him or her daily while you are reading the rest of this book. Write his or her name below and use it as a reminder during the next few weeks.

I commit to pray for:_____ Date:_____

Here are a few suggestions from the Bible about how to pray for your pre-Christian friends and peers. Sometimes you can make the loudest statement about Jesus without opening your mouth.

- **Pray** that the Lord will soften your friend's heart and prepare him by revealing his need for God (John 6:44).

- **Pray** that the Lord will use you as a powerful witness in this person's life (Acts 1:8).

- **Pray** that God will bring other Christians into this friend's life to be Christlike role models and prayer warriors for him. (Matthew 9:37–38).

- **Pray** that Satan will be prevented from pulling him away from the truth (Matthew 13:19).

- **Pray** that your friend will accept the Bible as the inspired Word of God (Romans 10:17).

- **Pray** that your friend will come to accept Jesus as both the Son of God and his Savior (Romans 10:9).

Now, put up a reminder on your bathroom mirror or a name on your screensaver. When you're done with this book, you may want to write this friend's name on a three-by-five-inch card and put it somewhere close to you as a continual reminder. You'll quickly find how difficult it is to remember to pray for someone consistently and earnestly every day. It's a good stretching exercise for the "prayer muscle."

And get excited! You may be the only Christian who has ever prayed for that person. It's a privilege for you and a gift for them. So take advantage of it, and be faithful to pray.

Jim Says: God wants us to talk to Him and ask Him for advice, just as I love it when my boys come to me for conversation or advice. Every once in a while my older boy, Christopher, seems exceptionally quiet when he comes home from school. When I ask him what he did at school, he'll answer, "Nothing" or "I forget" and walk away.

That makes me sad, but there's nothing I can do to make him talk. I just have to leave him alone, hoping that maybe later he'll open up and tell me if something is bothering him or what went on that day.

I think that's just how God feels. He wants us to talk to Him, but if we don't, He's not going to force us. He will just wait patiently until we are ready to turn to Him and open up. When we do, He is thrilled, all ears, and ready to do everything He knows is best for us.

3. Fast.

Contrary to popular belief among Christians, *fast* is not a four-letter word. Done right, fasting has a way of clearing out not only your stomach, but more importantly, your mind and spirit. We have had life-changing experiences while seeking God through times of fasting. It's a miraculous time of intimacy with the Lord that deserves its own book.

Sometimes Christians get a wrong idea about the purpose of fasting. They consider it a way to twist God's arm—like staging a hunger strike. They say they're entering an intense season of prayer about a certain issue, but they really may be trying to pressure God into doing something. Believe us, God can wait you out.

Fasting must have no agenda other than worship. You may hear from God during that time, but you may not. So don't let that be your motivation. You may decide to pray for a lost person during that time, but don't expect a prayer uttered during a fast to come with a double-your-money-back guarantee from God. Fast as an act of devotion, a freewill offering, just because you love Jesus with all your heart. Fast for intimacy with God and dependence on Him—no strings attached.

There are many spiritual disciplines we neglect for no better reason than that they are uncomfortable. We live in a "I want it; gotta have it now; I deserve it; be good to yourself; Just Do It" world. Self-denial isn't a part of our culture.

But we believe fasting is a spiritual discipline that must be introduced into the church before we can experience the breaking of Satan's power over the church, our nation, or the world. Bill Bright says that the power of fasting as it relates to prayer is the spiritual atomic bomb that the Lord has given us to destroy the strongholds of evil and usher in a great revival and spiritual harvest around the world.[3]

Here are some user-friendly ideas for fasting. (There is more information about fasting with prayer in appendix C.)

Practical Suggestions for Fasting

Choose what type of fast you want to do. Read about safe and wise fasting before starting.

- Juice fast: Drink juices of various fruits and vegetables.
- The Daniel fast: Eat just fruits and vegetables.
- Media fast: Turn off all television and radio and pray during that time.

Choose what length of fast you are most comfortable with. Start out with shorter fasts and build up to longer time periods. As with any diet or exercise, always consult your physician before engaging in an extended fast.

- One day a week
- One day to forty days—according to God's prompting
- One meal a day for forty days
- No TV or radio for a week, a month, etc.

Consider three essentials of fasting.
- Those whom God calls He equips for His purpose.
- God is able to do immeasurably more than we ask.
- Fasting without prayer is just a hunger strike.

Congratulations

You've made it through Part I!

And boy are you ready! You've cut out your excuses, conquered your fears, committed to a regimen of spiritual discipline, and concentrated your attention on the pre-Christians around you. And you even believe that not one of them is hopeless, don't you?

Salvation is the process of God reaching out, softening someone's heart, and opening his eyes. He's not in a hurry. He doesn't do it overnight. It takes days, months, even years. But be assured that once you start praying for someone, God will begin to speak to him in any number of ways.

Isn't it great that the Lord doesn't have to use us "despite ourselves"? As long as you make your relationship with the Lord your most important priority and you're committed to pray daily for your pre-Christian friends, you will start noticing the divine appointments that God arranges for you on a regular basis. If you're willing to talk about Jesus, He will bring you to the people who are ready to hear.

Now let's tell some stories.

---

1. Dietrich Bonhoeffer, *Life Together* (San Francisco: HarperSanFrancisco, 1954), 106.

2. Steve Sjogren, *Conspiracy of Kindness* (Ann Arbor, Mich.: Servant Publications, 1993), 22.

3. Dr. Bright has written some of the best resource material on this subject, and we highly recommend *The Power of Prayer and Fasting* and his pamphlet, *7 Basic Steps to Successful Fasting and Prayer.*

PART II

Three Stories
and a Word

CHAPTER FIVE

Their Story

*No one cares how much you know
until they know how much you care.*
UNKNOWN

Karen Says: I remember walking into my dorm room
when I first arrived at college and wondering what kind
of person my roommate would be. Would I have a dreadful year, or would I really like this stranger I was going to live with
for the next ten months?

The moment I met Debbie, I knew I'd be okay. When we started
asking each other questions, we found that we had much in common. As time went on, Debbie asked me questions about my spiritual life. At first I had no opinion about God, other than that I
believed in Him. But I began to think about Him more and more
and became curious about who He really is.

Debbie truly listened to my answers. Often she would come
back to me later with more specifics about something we had talked
about earlier. She was great at responding to my questions in a very
nonthreatening way. I learned to trust her with information, knowing that she wouldn't judge me or betray a confidence.

My trust and respect for Debbie eventually made me ready to embrace the Jesus she had told me so much about. And it was because she cared enough to listen and learn my story.

ONCE UPON A TIME...

We have a simple way to remember what we believe is the most effective approach to witnessing. We call it the three stories:

Their story

Your story

His story

Learning their story—a person's life story, or even just the story of his spiritual journey—is what earns you the right to then tell your story—how you met Jesus—and finally His story—God's plan of salvation.

This approach protects pre-Christians from having the gospel dumped on them with no sensitivity to their needs. If you use this approach, you will never have to worry about being an obnoxious Christian. Once all three stories have been told, you will know the person to whom you've witnessed, he will know you, and hopefully he will know Jesus.

In this chapter we are going to talk about the first story—their story. It's the way to develop a relationship, earn the right to be heard, and learn about the person to whom you're talking. You ask questions and listen to the answers instead of doing all the talking. You want to learn about his life, interests, needs, struggles, joys, spiritual journey, family, and church background, as well as his opinion, feelings, or belief about God.

88

WHAT ABOUT BOB?

Meet Bob. He works with you. You can't see inside Bob's heart, but from the evidence you've gathered so far, you're pretty sure he's not a Christian. You sure would like to talk to him about Jesus.

Okay, what do you do first? You would probably want to know a little bit about him, wouldn't you? I mean, does he know Jesus? Has he ever been exposed to the Bible? Does he have any interest in God? But you probably can't just come out and ask those things right off the top. You would probably start by asking about him, his family life, and his career goals.

Like most of us, Bob likes to talk about himself, so that's not a problem. He may not understand why, but he's getting the feeling that he really likes you. You're easy to talk to. You remind him of his mother or something. Finally, he realizes he's been talking the whole time, and he asks about you.

You and Bob talk back and forth comfortably. At an appropriate juncture, you bring up spiritual things. You know exactly how to approach the issue because you've taken the time to get to know Bob a little. He has sensed your genuine concern for him, and he has come to value your friendship, so he's less likely to respond rudely. In fact, by now he may be willing to enter into a serious, searching conversation with you about Jesus Christ.

How did this happen? It happened because you didn't hit Bob over the head with the gospel. You took the time to get to know him and to cultivate a friendship. And you started it all off by taking an interest in his personal story.

In our fast-paced, cybernetic culture we make a lot of acquaintances. But how many people do we really know? We try to keep in touch with as many friends as possible, but we often don't have time to hear about the details of our own spouse's day.

One of the downsides of our busy society is that we have

stopped paying attention to one another. With the advance of air travel and superhighways, we can be in the presence of almost anyone within hours. We may be able to get closer to one another faster, but in terms of intimacy, we are farther apart than ever. We have become shallow people overloaded with superficial acquaintances.

As Christians we should be different. God has said that His ways are not our ways. If we want to become effective in spreading the Good News to the people around us, we have to do it His way, not the world's way. We will not have an effective ministry if we just fax or e-mail the gospel to others without developing any personal relationship with them.

Years ago Brother Andrew, who smuggled Bibles into Communist countries, was asked why he took such dangerous risks. Why not just fly over these closed countries and drop crates of Bibles from airplanes instead of risking capture or even death by hand-delivering them across national borders? His response was, "The Bible says, 'Go ye into all nations,' not 'Dump ye into all nations.'" It's the same today. If we are to be effective witnesses, we have to meet people where they are, one-on-one, and love them to the Lord.

When talking to anyone about Jesus, be gracious enough to ask his name first, then pay attention. Take a moment to focus so you'll remember. There is no other word more precious to a person than his own name. Something as simple as remembering it can earn you the right to be heard. For at that moment, the conversation becomes personal.

People are looking for an ear to hear their cries for help. Unfortunately the unsaved do not always find it among Christians, because we are often talking when we should be listening. Dietrich Bonhoeffer went so far as to say: "He who can no longer listen to his brother will soon be no longer listening to God either."[1]

WHO ARE YOU, ANYWAY?

Only when we understand someone's situation can we most effectively present the personal message of the gospel to him. Jesus met many different needs, and each time He did, it was with a personal touch for a person who needed a personal message. Mark McCloskey points out that "people are not likely to accept a solution to a problem they don't believe they have, or listen to answers to questions they have never asked."[2]

If you have not listened to their story and learned what life path they've been on, how can you effectively meet their needs with the message of Christ? If you are telling a wealthy American woman that God is the one who meets our daily needs for food, she will probably disagree because she believes she meets that need herself. But if you ask her questions about her personal struggles and listen to what she has to say, you will be able to hear what her real needs are and then talk about how Jesus can meet them.

People are great at putting on happy faces of success. If you listen to them, though, you will frequently hear statements that reveal their hurts and struggles. If, on the other hand, you're not paying attention or are not willing to talk about difficult matters, you'll miss the opportunity to reach out to them with God's love.

We believe that when it comes to opportunities to tell someone about Jesus, there are no accidents. If an opportunity has come, there is a specific reason why God brought you to this person. You are suddenly in the middle of a divine appointment! Something about your personal experience is relevant or God would have brought someone else along. If you listen, you will know what part of your life to share with him.

Victorya Says: As a journalism major, I landed an opportunity to interview the star of a hit TV series. During the interview, he revealed in passing that his sister's spouse had murdered her. He had recently made a film in her memory. No one in the business knew this. But I was a very young and naive journalist. Out of discomfort, I immediately changed the subject, and I left it out of my report.

We miss crucial statements people make all the time by not paying attention or by avoiding the topic because it is out of our comfort zone.

5

WHICH PART DON'T YOU UNDERSTAND?

Have you ever said, "I'm so frustrated! My business partner won't ever accept the Lord. He's heard the plan of salvation—I told him myself! What will it take for him to get it?"

We can err in talking about Jesus if we are more concerned about getting the plan of salvation out than we are about the needs of the other person. It could be that the person wasn't ready to make a commitment to Christ. Remember, your job is only to move him one step closer to Jesus. But it could also be that your words didn't sink in because you hadn't earned the right to enter that deeply into the person's secret places.

Remember the three phases of the harvest? Getting to know a person's story is a large part of cultivating the relationship. If you try to skip that step, you reap a poor harvest.

You probably need to get to know your business partner or neighbor more personally or spend more time with him to build a friendship before he'll trust you. Jesus came to offer us a relationship with Him, and He commands us to do the same with others.

TOOL TIME TIPS

Here are some ideas about how to develop a relationship with a coworker, neighbor, or acquaintance whom God has placed on your heart.

- *Pray for opportunities.* Pray that God will lead you to people who are open to hear His message. You can meet spiritually responsive people through social relationships, professional events, at the gym, or in your neighborhood.

- *Be an open book.* Share openly, yet wisely, about your own life, and you will begin to find a reservoir of shared experiences with others. Speak freely about your faith and be bold in expressing your Christian perspective on issues, even though others may not agree. It may be a point of view that some people have never considered before.

- *Be a servant.* Look for opportunities to serve. You can buy someone a cup of coffee or clean his house when he's sick. Write an encouraging note. Call out of the blue to let someone know you're thinking of him.

- *Let others serve you.* If people ask to do something for you, let them. When we allow others to serve us, they experience the joy and blessing of "doing unto others." It also creates more intimacy between you.

- *Ask questions and then listen.* The best way to get to know people is to ask them lots of questions about themselves and then listen to their responses. If you're in a conversation and don't know what to do, ask one more question.

- *Speak their language.* If you are a computer fanatic, you have to consciously try not to use computer lingo when you talk to the average person who barely knows how to get on the Internet. It's

93

the same way with our Christian talk. Don't speak "Christianese" when you're building a relationship (more on this later).

- *Be patient.* Don't expect people to change overnight. It's God's job to change lives, not yours. You have to keep loving and loving and loving others until they are ready to embrace the source of your love.

Jim Says: Soon after we were married, Karen and I met a new Christian, Mikie, a studio singer and music producer. Because of the mutual love Mikie and I had for music, we became friends, but we couldn't have been more different.

Mikie was a former alcoholic, drug addict, and all-around not-so-nice guy. He came from a poor, blue collar, severely dysfunctional family who beat each other up and lied to and stole from one another. For whatever reason, he liked to hang out with Karen and me, even though he called us "geeks."

Some of Mikie's stories shocked us, and our naïveté dumbfounded him. Even though all of us were Americans, we spoke different languages and came from different cultures. There were times when we felt like we just weren't getting through to each other. But Karen and I knew we needed to understand Mikie's story before we could have an impact on his life. So we hung in there.

To our amazement, we soon developed a rich and loving respect for each other. We got past the barriers of language and lifestyle and learned about Mikie's heart. We helped each other grow as Christians, and Mikie, who taught us so much, is now a minister.

94

THE POWER OF QUESTIONS

The most powerful form of persuasion is to ask questions. Questions promote openness and vulnerability in conversations in a way that statements can't. Questions are easier for you and less threatening for the other person. They can also lead a conversation smoothly into spiritual discussions. The best teachers, lawyers, detectives, salesmen, doctors, and parents are those who have perfected the fine art of asking questions. And of course, Jesus was the Master of the probing question (Matthew 21:28–32; Luke 7:40–47).

Questions are powerful. They can go straight to the heart. Think of them as diagnostic tools that show you where someone stands in his journey. Once you've established where the patient is ailing, you can more expertly prescribe the treatment.

Never argue when you encounter resistance and hostility. We need to ask questions to find out why people feel the way they do and then be discerning about our response. Let your genuine love for God and for the person you are speaking to come through. Remember: It is not possible to argue a person *into* the kingdom, but it is possible to argue a person *away* from the kingdom!

Let's say you have just met someone at a party and are having a one-on-one conversation. You want to get to the point since you won't see him again until next year's office party. Let's look at how just asking questions can lead a conversation to Jesus. Notice the absence of statements.

- *It's nice to meet you, Bill. Have you lived in the area long?*
- *Do you have any family nearby?*
- *Do you get to see them often?*
- *How was it growing up there?*
- *Did your family do a lot together?*
- *Did your parents take you to church?*
- *How was that experience for you?*

95

- *Do you still go to church or think about going to church?*
- *Do you think what the church has to say about our society today is relevant?*
- *Do you believe God cares about you personally?*
- *Have you had some form of a personal encounter with God?*
- *What has been your spiritual journey?*
- *What do you think about Jesus?*
- *When Jesus said in the Bible, "I am the way, the truth, and the life and no one comes to the Father but by me," what do you think He meant?*
- *Did you know that you can have a personal relationship with God by knowing more about Jesus?*

Notice that with only a dozen or so questions you have gone from "Nice to meet you" to "Would you like to know Jesus personally?" These specific questions are not the focus. This exercise is just to demonstrate the power of questions. Being truly interested in the other person and listening to his answers are the key to successfully transitioning into a conversation about Jesus. Questions are your passkey.

Karen Says: Once when Jim and I were at an industry party, Jim got into a conversation with a woman named Sheila. She was a "spiritual" person, but she had no understanding of the Bible or Jesus. At one point Jim asked her a question: "What do you think Jesus meant when He said, 'I am the way, the truth, and the life. No one can come to the Father except through me'?"

Sheila was instantly upset: "I can't believe you're interpreting it that way." Jim explained that he wasn't interpreting anything. Those were just the words that Jesus Himself had said. Sheila became very anxious and said, "If you insist on interpreting the Bible like that I just can't talk to you any more about it." And she walked away. One question revealed a lot. Her actions told us clearly that she was angry toward God, and we then knew how to pray for her.

IT'S A WRAP

If you tell someone what you think he needs to hear before you know his story, how are you different from a door-to-door salesman? We get enough solicitations already. You can't just throw out a canned speech and expect results. You've got to be sincerely interested in the other person. What more can you learn about him? What are his needs?

Taking the time and effort to discover to whom you're talking does two things: First, it shows you are concerned about him for who he is, which will cause him to lower his defenses and be more open to hear about Jesus. Second, it helps you see how best to present the gospel to him. Many people we know pay hundreds of dollars an hour to have someone listen to "their story." And many professionally trained listeners respond with only "I'm sorry, our time is up. I'll see you at week." You may be the only person in your friend's life who has the answer to his dilemma.

So, ask questions, listen, care about the other person, learn details about his life, and never assume that somebody has it all together. The Lord knows we don't.

1.   Dietrich Bonhoeffer, *Life Together* (San Francisco: HarperSanFrancisco, 1954), 97–8.

2.   Mark McCloskey, *Tell It Often, Tell It Well* (San Bernardino, Calif.: Here's Life Publishers, 1985), 36.

CHAPTER SIX

Your Story

*Always be prepared to give an answer to everyone who asks
you to give the reason for the hope that you have.*

1 PETER 3:15B (NIV)

Karen Says: Lynette was taking our class. She told us that
she had once been asked to give her testimony at a church.
She was insecure, fearing she had nothing exciting to share
because she had come from a stable family. She had no radical conversion story. But the preacher urged her to try anyway, so she did.

When she was done, the preacher thanked her, but told her that
her story had been a bit boring. Lynette was extremely embarrassed
and discouraged. She vowed never to tell anyone her story again.

In our class years later, Lynette told us how reluctant she was to
tell her story again. We encouraged her to tell us anyway, and the
next week she came in with an amazing story. She expressed the
simplicity of God's love and how it had brought her great joy and
hope. The rest of the class was truly moved.

As Lynette's story unfolded, it was far from boring. She was
telling us that she had grown up in a functional home. To most of
Americans that in itself is a miraculous story! What we heard in her
story about her loving home life was how a faithful God had poured

out His blessings on her. It made us want to know more about Him. And isn't that the purpose of a personal testimony?

No Story Is Boring

Everyone has a story! What's yours? If you have never sat down and written out your spiritual testimony in chronological order, when you do, you'll be amazed at how God has been working in your life. No testimony is boring. Your story is unique and fascinating, and whenever you tell it, it will be relevant and potentially life changing for the listener.

A personal testimony is the most nonthreatening way to tell an unbeliever why Jesus is important to you. It allows you to be open about your life while giving God the glory. You can rave about the power of Jesus to transform a life, yet even a hostile audience will listen because you're not asking anything of them. It's also a powerful story because it is unique to you and because it describes one instance of the miracle of salvation.

We know that our faith is based on the divine truth and accuracy of the Bible. We also know that we will encounter skeptics who like to argue that the Bible has been changed over and over again as it has been passed down through time. Your story, however, is as fresh and modern as the morning paper. Oral tradition has not transformed it into a myth with bigger-than-life characters, as some claim the Bible has been. Your story is compelling because it's personal and experiential. You can prove it's true because you were there! It can't be refuted.

If you are convinced that being a Christian is the best way to live, you shouldn't hold back the Good News. If you are passionate about your relationship with God, your story will be so infectious that it will cause others to want the same thing. But you need to be prepared to express it clearly and concisely.

Jim Says: A few years ago, Karen and I were invited to a dinner party at the house of a friend who wanted to get her spiritually eclectic circle of friends together to learn about one another's beliefs. We arrived a bit late. When we walked through the door our hostess introduced us as her "fundamentalist friends." Not a great way to be labeled at a Hollywood party! But we just made a joke and walked on in.

After the meal our hostess said, "Now let's go around the table and all of us tell what we think about Jesus." How's that for dinner table conversation? Karen and I listened to every imaginable opinion about Jesus—from His being a crutch or myth, to a prophet or good man, to a political ploy. It was fascinating.

Then the man across the table turned to me and said, "Jim, in three minutes or less, tell us what you think about Jesus." When that man asked me to give the reason for the hope that is in me, I had a platform to tell my story, and I was ready. I told it on the spot, adapting it to the situation. Because the main points were so familiar, I was sure I'd left nothing out.

If I had not prepared it beforehand, I might have missed a tremendous opportunity to lift up the truth to a group of people who were searching for Jesus, but who might otherwise not have had the opportunity to hear about Him.

6

The Three-Minute Testimony

Your story is simply the account of how God has changed your life. If Jesus is your Lord and Savior, then surely He has done miraculous things for you. People are looking for evidence that God exists and that He is personally involved in individual lives. You can't make God appear on the spot to prove His existence, but you can certainly point straight to Him by talking about how He has worked in your life.

Even if you can't remember when you haven't known God, and rockets and fireworks weren't part of your conversion experience, we guarantee that you have had times of need when God has carried you through. Those are the experiences you need to talk about. When you tell of God's faithfulness to you, He gets the glory, and your story moves the listener one step closer to Him.

Jim Says: I was at a party telling a man my personal story, which included being raised in a functional family and being a virgin until I got married. He said, "That's the most bizarre thing I've ever heard. I think I need to write a book about you."

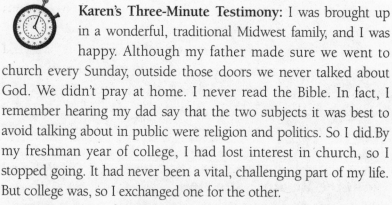

Karen's Three-Minute Testimony: I was brought up in a wonderful, traditional Midwest family, and I was happy. Although my father made sure we went to church every Sunday, outside those doors we never talked about God. We didn't pray at home. I never read the Bible. In fact, I remember hearing my dad say that the two subjects it was best to avoid talking about in public were religion and politics. So I did.By my freshman year of college, I had lost interest in church, so I stopped going. It had never been a vital, challenging part of my life. But college was, so I exchanged one for the other.

My roommate, however, did go to church. In fact, Debbie was the most amazing person I had ever met. She had had a horrible upbringing: two alcoholic parents, a father who committed suicide (whom *she* found dead), and a little brother who was killed by a car while she was taking a walk with him. Compared to her, I had it all, and yet my life was going haywire that year.

Despite her background, Debbie was more peaceful than I was and seemed more stable. She was a listener and seemed to respond with wisdom beyond her years. I remember asking her how she handled life. The answers she gave me came from the Bible. She explained how God cares about every detail of my life. I found myself enjoying our talks, and I quickly saw that in this time of searching, confusion, and poor choices, my life was empty in comparison to hers. I wanted more out of my life. I believed she had it, and the "it" had to be God. As she explained it, I needed to have a personal relationship with Jesus Christ. It was beginning to make sense.

By the end of my freshman year, I had friends at both ends of the spiritual spectrum. I had a small group of solid, loving Christian friends, and I had wild friends who lived in the world of drugs, drinking, and sex. Though my wild friends were exciting for the moment, I saw that my lasting friends were for the most part Christians. And they were also fun! I knew in my heart the time was coming when I would have to make a choice.

One beautiful afternoon in May, while walking across campus, I decided to make a deal with God and try out the beliefs of my Christian friends. I remembered a Bible verse Debbie had quoted: "If you confess with your mouth that Jesus is Lord and believe in your heart that God raised him from the dead, you will be saved" (Romans 10:9).

I told God that I would let Jesus take control of my life and become my personal Savior—on the condition that I would never have to tell anyone about my decision. I definitely did not want to become a missionary to Africa. I didn't even want to tell Debbie about it. If something supernatural really happened to me, I'd see if Debbie would be able to notice on her own.

After my next class I came back to our dorm room, and the first thing Debbie asked was, "What's different about you?" I said, "Nothing" and went to do my homework. Later that evening she asked me again. The next morning she wouldn't let me out of the room until I told her if I had become a Christian. At that moment I knew a miracle had happened. God had taken over my life and had immediately gone to work.

A month later, I told both my mom and my grandmother about my decision to become a born-again Christian. They both asked to become Christians, too. Eight years later, my husband and I realized that we were missionaries—not in Africa—but in Hollywood. Soon we began teaching a class on "How To Talk about Jesus without Freaking Out." So much for never telling anyone! That's when I realized I had truly become a new creature, because the only thing I couldn't *stop* talking about was Jesus.

6

One advantage of preparing a personal testimony is that it makes you realize how God has been at work on your behalf. Sometimes we forget, don't we? When you sit down and reflect on how Jesus has reached out and touched your life, you will be moved to worship. You will see God working to turn your innermost struggles into victories one at a time. You'll also be reminded of how faithful God has been.

This is sometimes hard for people who have very painful pasts. No one likes dredging up bad memories. Nevertheless, by writing out the steps of your journey, it's ultimately healing to see that Jesus has pulled you out of the muck and is slowly working incredible changes in you, through you, and for you.

Another reason your personal testimony is powerful is because it's a story. Have you ever realized how much of the Bible is told in stories? Teachers and parents teach children principles by telling them stories. Preachers make their points with stories from Scripture. Jesus Himself taught with stories. His parables were highly effective in communicating His message.

A story can convey information in a way that forces the listener to respond emotionally—and thus remember the storyteller's point. The story is a creation of God, a gift from Him that we should use to reach a lost world.

Victorya's Three-Minute Testimony: I had the privilege of being raised in a strong Christian home. From birth all the way through college I attended a small church in Long Beach, California. As long as I can remember, Jesus has been very real to me.

However, I was also very insecure growing up. I didn't know how to be popular at school, and I was terrified of rejection, confrontation, and conflict. I thought of God as an extremely strict, unbending judge. My young mind focused on sermons about God's wrath; I didn't understand His grace. I lived according to a list of dos and don'ts, and I deduced that Christians had to be perfect. If you fail, you go to hell—plain and simple. I was utterly terrified of messing up for fear that I'd die in some accident before I could repent.

Therefore, in sheer terror, I did everything I could to be perfect. I was a goody-two-shoes walking the straight and narrow—but I was driven by guilt. I knew Jesus loved me, but I was terrified that I wasn't good enough for Him. I was sure He would reject me for my failures. Throughout high school and college, I was a perfect little angel, terrified of upsetting God, my church, or my parents.

By age twenty-three, however, I couldn't take the fear or stomachaches anymore. Finally I moved out on my own, to Los Angeles to be near my work. I also "rebelled" for the first time in my life. I started dancing and no longer believed that drinking a glass of wine would send me to hell.

Though I had not been popular with boys, except as a "buddy," now I was determined to learn to fit in and be accepted by men. I got caught up in searching for physical perfection. I was convinced that if I just walked the walk, talked the talk, and learned how to be beautiful, men would fall in love with me. It worked: Dating lots of men became a busy pastime. But it was empty. There was quantity but not quality. By my midtwenties, dating had left me feeling shallow and unfulfilled.

I still loved Jesus and attended church every Sunday, but I was becoming distant from God. And the separation and guilt really got to me. Once you've known the Lord and walked with Him, it's hard to be a good sinner!

I learned several valuable lessons during that painful period in my life. I learned that Jesus loves me even when I'm ugly and no one seems to care. I learned that He loves me when I fail Him by doing what I know is wrong. And I learned that even though I ran from Him, Jesus kept tugging at my heart and pulling me back, just as He said He would: "Never will I leave you; never will I forsake you" (Hebrews 13:5, NIV).

Most importantly, I began to learn about God's grace. Ephesians 2:8–9 (NIV) is very precious to me: "For it is by grace you have been saved, through faith—and this not from yourselves, it is the gift of God—not by works, so that no one can boast." This reminds me that trying to be perfect, angelic Christians does not save us. We are saved by accepting the free gift of God.

6

It's a Setup!

Some of you may be saying right now, "Hey, isn't it contrived to have your testimony *prepared?* Whatever happened to spontaneity and speaking straight from the heart? Doesn't the Spirit give us the words we need to speak?"

Consider this: Would you go to an important business meeting without being thoroughly prepared? Would you walk unprepared into a courtroom for a trial? Would you show up to perform on opening night without your lines memorized?

Of course the Holy Spirit moves us and leads us in our conversations about Christ. But it's our responsibility to use what the Lord gives us in the best possible way. We prepare for important meetings; we need to prepare to give an account of our faith as well. Studying and memorizing Scripture not only edifies our souls, it also brings the words to mind at the appropriate moment. Just as we try to memorize God's story from the Bible, we should memorize the story of our life.

Has anyone ever asked you why your life seemed so different from his? Did you answer well? Did you give God the credit? Or did you find yourself caught off-guard, unprepared to give an effective response? There have been times when each of us has walked away from a conversation kicking ourselves because we said nothing. If you have a three-minute testimony prepared, you will never go through that again.

Your story is just that: your story. There's no pressure, and you won't have to memorize a monologue word-for-word like you did when you had to recite the Gettysburg Address in school. You just have to memorize a few main points. In the next chapter we talk about the ABCs of salvation: admit, believe, confess. An acronym like this or some other memory device will help you remember the key points of your story.

Once you have an outline prepared, you can spontaneously adapt it to any situation. Most likely you'll never give your testimony exactly as you wrote it out. This is your story planted in your heart so that it's ready to be told at any moment for the rest of your life.

No, it is not contrived to know your testimony ahead of time.

Jim Says: One Sunday we were talking to our Sunday school class about preparing a three-minute testimony. Afterwards, a friend who is a police officer offered us a fresh perspective.

He said that when someone is called on to testify as a witness in court, he can only speak about what he has personally seen, heard, or experienced. The witness can't say what someone else heard or saw, and he can't say what he assumes to be true. The evidence considered in a court of law is only an account of the witness's personal experience and how it affected him (cf. 1 John 1:1–4).

That's exactly what you're doing when you prepare your testimony. You are testifying about your personal encounter with God and how it impacted you. That's all the jury wants to hear when they are searching for answers. Therefore, you have to be ready to testify clearly and concisely when you are called to the stand. It's then up to the jury to decide if what you're saying is true.

6

Your Spiritual Autobiography

Writing a personal testimony is really very simple. It's merely giving shape to a story that has already been written. You just need to organize it in a presentable form.

Your purpose is to let others know what Christ has done in your life. We suggest that you make your story approximately three minutes in length because that's the average time you'll be able to hold a listener's undivided attention. When appropriate, you can make it longer, giving a fuller explanation or embellishing it with details. However, it's much more difficult to condense than to expand it. Keep it short enough so that you can communicate the facts to someone who's waiting for a cab or in line to pay at the register.

Explain your story in such a way that others will identify with your past and present experiences, not just your conversion. You need to show the transformation in your life, whether it is subtle or dramatic. Show how your life is a fulfillment of God's promise that, "If anyone is in Christ, he is a new creation; the old has gone, the new has come!" (2 Corinthians 5:1, NIV). Remember that we're all recovering humans; we're still works in process. It's not over 'til it's over.

The format is simple: B.C. Year Zero, and A.D.

- **Before Christ (B.C.)**
  Your spiritual journey began with the time *before* you had any knowledge of Jesus Christ (B.C.: Before Christ). Talk about your life as an unbeliever or about how you grew up in a Christian home.

- **Meeting Christ (Year Zero)**
  Then there came a time when you were introduced to Jesus, and you knew you had to choose whether or not you were going to believe Jesus Christ is who He said He is. Year Zero is the time you *met Christ* and consciously chose to follow Him—the moment of your conversion. Talk about when you made a personal commitment to Christ.

- **After Christ (A.D.)**
  A.D. stands for *anno Domini,* Latin for "Year of the Lord." After you accepted Christ into your life, He began transforming you. That part of the story will never be over, but at any given point

109

in time you are experiencing victories or seeing evidence that God is working. Every year after your salvation is a year of the Lord. Talk about what Jesus has done in your life since He changed you.

Now that you have a simple outline, find a theme that is characteristic of your life. As you think over your life, B.C. and A.D., does a pattern emerge? Is there a lesson you never seem to learn or a direction He keeps pointing you? Look for a thread that unifies your story.

This doesn't have to be anything profound. Just pick something personal that will be of interest to pre-Christians and provide a structure for your story. The theme you choose should allow you to bring in areas of your personal struggle, growth, and ultimate victory in your life.

There will be more than one theme to talk about in your life and more than one way to string together its main points. Choose two or three themes. Once you get the hang of applying the same points to different themes, you'll be able to do it in a witnessing situation. Keep it simple and flexible.

EXAMPLES OF THEMES FOR YOUR PERSONAL TESTIMONY

- addictions
- arrogance
- bulimia
- depression
- disappointments
- dysfunctional family
- life goals
- loneliness
- personal successes
- self-reliance
- spiritual emptiness
- unmet expectations

The easiest way to put your personal testimony together is to first write out your spiritual autobiography. Your first draft may be five pages or fifty. However long, it's worth the exercise to write it out. Think about the three phases of your spiritual life and its major themes.

There will be many variations on this basic outline. If you grew up in a wonderful Christian home, you may never be able to pinpoint a specific conversion experience. You may have just *always* known Jesus. Think back to the time when you chose to follow Christ apart from your family's influence. Or you may have recommitted your life to Christ after you had walked away from the God of your youth. Perhaps you had a dramatic conversion experience, but later turned away from Jesus. Then, years later, you turned to the Lord again and made an even deeper commitment. There are many other possible scenarios.

The bottom line is that you clearly state how Jesus Christ has changed your life and why you have chosen to continue letting Him be Lord. Tell when you accepted Him as your Savior, how He's changed you, and what the tangible results have been in your life.

Go ahead and write down your outline. We'll wait.

Outline for Your Personal Testimony

• **Introduction:** Establish common ground with your listener or define the main theme of your story.

• **B.C.:** Describe your life before you knew Christ or your experience of growing up in a Christian home.

• **Year Zero:** Describe your conversion experience.

• **A.D.:** Describe your life after you became a Christian and tell how the Lord has changed or is continuing to change you.

Done? Okay, after you have written the blueprint, expand it into about three minutes' worth of text. When you have it written out, read it aloud and time yourself. Then tell it to a friend or family member, asking him to comment on the clarity and flow of the story. Practice it out loud until it becomes a natural part of your life.

We encourage you to memorize your story—or at least your outline. But please do not memorize it word-for-word like a speech. If you do, you may feel you have to say every word you've written down in the order that you wrote them. You'll be afraid of flubbing it; you'll be rigidly locked into a spiel, unable to alter it even when the situation changes; and you'll sound like you're giving a sales pitch. That will make your own life story seem canned and contrived. Not good. What you're striving for as you practice your story is adaptability and freshness.

In Acts 26:1–23 the Bible offers us a perfect example of a three-minute testimony. Paul is making his case before King Agrippa. Here we find a beautiful example of a well-constructed and powerful testimony of who Paul was before he met Christ, how he met Jesus personally, and who he became as he faithfully followed Christ. Amazingly, it takes about three minutes to read Paul's story.

Paul's Three-Minute Testimony (Acts 26:1–23): "Then Agrippa said to Paul, 'You may speak in your defense.'

"So Paul, with a gesture of his hand, started his defense: 'I am fortunate, King Agrippa, that you are the one hearing my defense against all these accusations made by the Jewish leaders, for I know you are an expert on Jewish customs and controversies. Now please listen to me patiently!

"As the Jewish leaders are well aware, I was given a thorough Jewish training from my earliest childhood among my own people and in Jerusalem. If they would admit it, they know that I have been a member of the Pharisees, the strictest sect of our religion. Now I am on trial because I am looking forward to the fulfillment of God's promise made to our ancestors. In fact, that is why the twelve tribes of Israel worship God night and day, and they share the same hope I have. Yet, O king, they say it is wrong for me to have this hope! Why does it seem incredible to any of you that God can raise the dead?

"I used to believe that I ought to do everything I could to oppose the followers of Jesus of Nazareth. Authorized by the leading priests, I caused many of the believers in Jerusalem to be sent to prison. And I cast my vote against them when they were condemned to death. Many times I had them whipped in the synagogues to try to get them to curse Christ. I was so violently opposed to them that I even hounded them in distant cities of foreign lands.

"One day I was on such a mission to Damascus, armed with the authority and commission of the leading priests. About noon, Your Majesty, a light from heaven brighter than the sun shone down on me and my companions. We all fell down, and I heard a voice saying to me in Aramaic, 'Saul, Saul, why are you persecuting me? It is hard for you to fight against my will.'

"'Who are you, sir?' I asked.

"And the Lord replied, 'I am Jesus, the one you are persecuting. Now stand up! For I have appeared to you to appoint you as my servant and my witness. You are to tell the world about this experience and about other times I will appear to you. And I will protect you from both your own people and the Gentiles. Yes, I am going to send you to the Gentiles, to open their eyes so they may turn from darkness to light, and from the power of Satan to God. Then they will receive forgiveness for their sins and be given a place among God's people, who are set apart by faith in me.'

"And so, O King Agrippa, I was not disobedient to that vision from heaven. I preached first to those in Damascus, then in

Jerusalem and throughout all Judea, and also to the Gentiles, that all must turn from their sins and turn to God—and prove they have changed by the good things they do. Some Jews arrested me in the Temple for preaching this, and they tried to kill me. But God protected me so that I am still alive today to tell these facts to everyone, from the least to the greatest. I teach nothing except what the prophets and Moses said would happen—that the Messiah would suffer and be the first to rise from the dead as a light to Jews and Gentiles alike."

What an encouraging three-minute testimony—taken directly from Scripture. Did you find the B.C., Year Zero, and A.D. sections?

Even Paul never told his story the same way twice. In fact, we find bits and pieces of his spiritual autobiography throughout the New Testament. He said what was appropriate to the circumstances at hand. You are not likely to tell your story the same way twice, either, but you should know all the important points so that you're prepared to share it with those the Lord brings into your path.

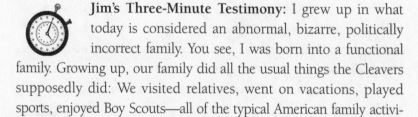

Jim's Three-Minute Testimony: I grew up in what today is considered an abnormal, bizarre, politically incorrect family. You see, I was born into a functional family. Growing up, our family did all the usual things the Cleavers supposedly did: We visited relatives, went on vacations, played sports, enjoyed Boy Scouts—all of the typical American family activities. My parents also took me to church.

However, growing up in church doesn't make you a Christian, any more than growing up in a garage makes you a car. When I was a child, church meant flannel boards, punch, and cookies. In junior

115

high, it was camp, hanging out, and girls.

In high school I started asking questions about life as well as about girls. I always knew about Jesus and sang all the songs and hymns about Him. It always seemed logical to me that if God wanted to communicate with us, He would send us a messenger that was part God and part man. I had also learned by watching my parents that love required sacrifice. Reading the Bible taught me that God loves us so much that He sent His Son to Earth so that whoever believed and put their trust in Him would have an eternal and abundant life (John 3:16). Growing up, I always believed this was the truth.

The gospel of Jesus made sense to me, and in my early teens, I decided that my commitment to Jesus was truly my own and not just something my family was passing on to me.

The Bible says that the mistakes of one generation are passed down to the next as curses, but "the blessings of the righteous are a thousandfold through the generations." I see many people stuck in a downward spiral, repeating the patterns their family passed on to them (i.e. alcoholism, anger, sexual dysfunctions). Only the grace of God can rescue them. I received the blessings of my parents, grand-parents, and great-grandparents, who chose to follow God's truth. And then I embraced them for myself.

Today, I'm the father of two wonder boys, who have the world's greatest mom. God has allowed all of us the freedom to make our own choices, and I'm aware that the choices I make directly affect their innocent lives. I also clearly see that love takes sacrifice. I still have daily struggles, and I don't always succeed in all areas of my life, but with God's help I press on and continue to love Jesus.

Just as my boys have the freedom to love me, God has given us the choice to love Him. I don't want to force my children to love me any more than God wants that for His children. This is what the Bible calls being created in the image of God. So, every night I repeat to my little boys the same thing my mother said to me—the twenty-third Psalm. "Because the Lord is my shepherd, I have everything I need...." It's my desire to pass this "bizarre" blessing on to my children and their children's children in turn. With Jesus' help, it will be so.

Christianese

Every culture and subculture has its own language, terminology, and buzzwords. Hollywood has its jargon, just as computer technicians or gymnasts have theirs. When we tell our church friends about a "MOW overnight," their eyes glaze over. When Jim tells Karen he's having trouble with his "scuzzy connections," she just laughs. These terms are examples of specialized lingo that estrange us from outsiders. We do this as Christians as well.

Victorya Says: Joe was a pre-Christian who accepted an invitation to join a Bible study. He attended the study faithfully each week, but he was very quiet. One day after the study he finally spoke to the leader. He said he was enjoying it very much and really liked the topics of discussion, but there was one question that kept gnawing at him. He wanted to know what "the Word" was. He kept hearing everyone talk about it, but he didn't know what it could be. He thought it was probably a secret code known only to the initiated. What was that magic word?

Many Christians spend so much time with other believers that they start speaking "Christianese." It's a dialect of English that is found mostly inside the confines of American churches. It flourishes where Christians spend too much time isolated from the outside world. Sometimes Christians outside a particular denomination can't even understand it.

At best, our cliquish terms are a hindrance to effectively communicating the gospel. At worst, they can turn off our pre-Christian friends. You need to be careful with your choice of words around them. You want to be understood, right? As you work out your story, be sure to keep an eye out for Christianese.

Here is a sampling of terms that Christians use, but which outsiders often do not understand. We challenge you to either define them as you use them or choose more culturally relevant terms to replace them. We have given you definitions of the terms to help you come up with clear, short phrases to explain or replace each word. You may discover that you have never known the meaning of some of the words you've been using for years!

- **BORN AGAIN:** Accepting Jesus as your Lord and Savior and receiving a new spiritual life; spiritual birth; to become alive spiritually; to become a new creation as a result of Christ's sacrifice (payment) for your sins.

- **FAITH:** Blind trust or belief; choosing to believe in something without having tangible proof; taking God at His word; Forsaking All, I Trust Him (F.A.I.T.H.).

- **GOSPEL:** The Good News about Jesus; the chance to be reconciled with God through Christ's sacrifice. Note that this word also refers to the four biblical accounts of the life of Jesus—the *Gospels* of Matthew, Mark, Luke, and John.

- **GRACE:** God's inexplicable kindness; unconditional forgiveness; a gift we don't deserve.

- **INVITE JESUS INTO YOUR HEART:** To ask God to have a personal relationship with you; to ask Jesus to take control of your life; to your trust Jesus to forgive your sins; to accept Christ as your own personal Savior.

- **JUSTIFIED:** Acquitted in the court of heaven; forgiven; made right; guilty but forgiven; excused; made **JUST** as **IF I** never sinn**ED**.

- **LOST:** Without Christ in one's life; estranged from God; hopeless; off course; needing to be found or saved; trying to find eternal life and hope.

- **REDEEMED:** Freed from bondage; bought back with a price; rescued; released upon payment of a ransom.

- **REPENT:** A military term meaning to make a 180-degree turn; to ask forgiveness; to make an about-face; to turn away from a wrong behavior; to change one's mind and actions.

- **RIGHTEOUS:** In right standing before God; declared legally perfect; aligned to the standard; upright; pure at heart; blameless.

- **SALVATION:** The result of being saved; the promise of eternal life; being rescued from eternal death in hell; to receive spiritual life; deliverance from the consequences of one's sinful actions (see also *saved*).

- **SAVED:** To be rescued from a deserved penalty; to be given eternal life; to have eternal fellowship with God; to have a relationship with Christ; to not go to hell.

- **SHARE:** To talk to someone; to express an opinion or relate an experience; to offer information; to open up your heart to someone; to talk confidentially.

- **SIN:** Originally an archery term meaning "to miss the mark"; wrongdoing; imperfect deeds that separate a person from God; disobedience to God's divine law; self-centeredness; anything less than perfect; choosing one's own way instead of God's way.

- **TRUTH:** Ultimate reality; the absolutes given to man through the Bible; Jesus as the personification of truth.

- **WALK:** One's relationship with Christ; a spiritual journey; step-by-step, day-by-day relationship with Jesus Christ; the Christian life.

- **THE WORD:** The Bible, both Old and New Testaments; the Scriptures; Jesus.

How many of us ever think about how we come across to unbelievers? Think about what it's like when you're listening to someone using jargon you don't know. They might as well be speaking Mandarin. Listen to yourself through the world's ears.

Your goal is to include people in the things of God, not exclude them. Be sure everyone to whom you talk about Jesus understands what you're saying. Learn to convey the essentials of Christianity in everyday English, not Christianese. Ask the Lord to give you the simplest, clearest words possible for the benefit of your pre-Christian friends. Like Paul, become all things to all people so that some may be saved (1 Corinthians 9:22).

Helpful Hints

Now that you have cut the Christianese from your three-minute testimony, here are some additional hints for preparing your story.

Speak to God first.

Ask Him to speak through you. Ask the Holy Spirit to give you wisdom and guidance as you write.

Use at least one Scripture.

Pick a verse that holds a promise for you. As you tell your story, it's good to include God's Word and tell how it has impacted you. Some people quote Jeremiah 29:11: "'For I know the plans I have for you,' says the LORD. 'They are plans for good and not for disaster, to give you a future and a hope.'" Romans 10:9 and John 3:16 are other favorites.

Even very early in your Christian experience you should have some verse of Scripture that helps define your walk with the Lord—your "life verse." Find that verse and include it in your story. Using the wondrous Word of God will be stronger testimony than a thousand good words of your own.

Avoid negative talk.

Avoid using language that will distract from your message. This includes negative comments about people, organizations, or denominations. It's okay to mention those topics if it's helpful in establishing a connection between you and your listener—if your friend is from the same denomination, for example—but don't offend him by speaking negatively about anyone or anything. Why would someone want to embrace a hateful or judgmental religion? Christians need to be different.

Use the name of Jesus.

It's important to lift up the name of Jesus. *God* is a safer word to use these days, for many people embrace some concept of god—a mother-god; god as a power within us; a god-energy. This is especially true in a culture in which many people think they are god.

Jesus, however, is the cornerstone, the dividing line among all religions, beliefs, and sects. He is the only one in all of history to claim, "I am the way, the truth, and the life. No one can come to the Father except through me" (John 14:6). We have to let people know that we follow Jesus Christ, not just some generic divinity.

Just Do It

All right, you're ready. Take out pen and paper and start working on a three-minute account of your spiritual journey. Pray as you plan and write it. Don't worry about what kind of writer you are; just be honest about how Jesus has changed your life. Focus on your major experiences, decisions, struggles, and victories.

God's faithfulness in your life is going to surprise you—so much so that you'll be bursting to tell someone else about it! You are a trophy of God's grace. He has exerted His resurrection power in your life. Stand up and tell your story!

CHAPTER SEVEN

His Story

*Jesus replied, "I assure you, unless you are born again,
you can never see the Kingdom of God."*
JOHN 3:3

Karen Says: As a new Christian, though I was on fire for Christ, I still didn't want to talk about Jesus with other people. Remember my bargain with God? Nevertheless, I allowed myself to respond to a challenge given by the head of a ministry on campus: to go out and boldly share my faith with the students.

I was scared to death, but I wanted to prove to my Christian friends that I could handle it. So out of guilt and pride, I ventured out onto campus looking for the right person to talk to about Jesus. I saw someone coming and mustered up my courage. With great embarrassment, I tried to interest him in the plan of salvation by fumbling around with concepts I had just learned.

It quickly turned into one of the worst experiences of my life. The poor guy left, untouched and clearly unimpressed. I broke down crying, thinking, *If this is what it means to be a Christian, maybe I made a mistake. This is not for me!*

A month later, I went home to Chicago for the summer. My parents' marriage was falling apart, and I was beside myself with grief. Out of a desperate concern for my mom, I hesitantly told her about my spiritual journey during the past year. I told her I wouldn't have made it through another year in college if I hadn't given Jesus control of my life. I explained how I'd asked Him to take over for me because I wasn't doing such a great job. I suggested that she ask Jesus to help her in her despair.

Mom immediately agreed and asked me more questions about salvation. She wanted to know what it really meant to be a Christian and how to embrace Jesus. Within a short time she said that she, too, wanted to become a Christian. Again I fumbled for the right words, and together we prayed to bring her into the kingdom. We ended our conversation crying and hugging. I remember thinking, *Now this must be what being a Christian is all about.* It was one of the most powerful and memorable times of my life.

What made the difference? I told both people the same story. I flubbed it both times. I wasn't any more knowledgeable a month later than I had been that day on campus. But one conversation ended in disaster and the other in joy.

What was different was my motivation. The first time, I was telling God's story because I felt obligated to my friends, and I wanted to prove to them and myself that I was "good." The second time, I was telling Jesus' story to my mom because my heart was breaking for her, and I believed that He was the only one who could help her.

To Go Boldly

We have walked you through the first two steps of sharing your faith: their story—getting to know the person you're talking to by listening—and your story—letting him get to know you by effectively sharing your own spiritual journey. Now we get to where the rubber meets the spiritual road: His story!

Most commonly referred to as the plan of salvation, His story is the account of who God is and what He has done—and still does—to offer us a way to live with Him forever. "I take no pleasure in the death of anyone, declares the Sovereign LORD. Repent and live!" (Ezekiel 18:32, NIV). God wants "everyone to be saved and to understand the truth" (1 Timothy 2:4). His story is at the heart of our responsibility to "go and make disciples of all nations" (Matthew 28:19).

This is the toughest step to take and the hardest story to tell. One of the most difficult tasks for a Christian is to look someone in the eye and tell him God's plan for his life. *The* most difficult is to tell someone that he needs Jesus!

No sooner do you determine to witness to someone than you start hearing a strong, annoying voice telling you that you're going to look stupid or that you'll say the wrong thing. The voice questions your right even to talk about Jesus. "Not now," it says, "wait until you've completed that witnessing book you're reading. Plenty of time later." All the excuses we talked about in chapter 1 and all the fears we discussed in chapter 2—and others we haven't mentioned—will parade through your mind. *No! You'll offend this person! You'll be branded a fanatic. You might lose your job. He's not ready for this right now.*

The voice belongs to Satan, and although he may sound convincing, the bottom line is that Satan is a liar. Once you begin to recognize his lies, you'll be well on your way to gaining victory over them. Then you will go boldly where no frightened Christian has ever gone before!

Even when you stop listening to Satan's lies and decide to talk about Jesus, you may still be a bit shaky. It happens to us, too! Never mind that we teach a class on witnessing; at times we still get nervous and fumble for the right words when we explain the plan of salvation. We can tell His story only because our hearts break for the person and because we believe Jesus is the only one who can help.

You have to come to this place as well. Your heartbreak over the other person's condition will catapult you over your fears. Who would run into an empty burning building? No one. But what if you knew there was a baby in there? All of a sudden you would forget your terror and be willing to brave the danger because a precious life is at stake.

Who would run into an empty burning building? No one. But what if you knew there was a baby in there?

So it is with witnessing. When you see the lostness of the person you're talking to—his misery, emptiness, and woundedness—and how precariously he's balancing on the edge of eternal suffering, your fears will begin to recede. A precious soul is at stake.

That realization will motivate you to risk sharing the most earth-shaking truth of all time.

But beware! When your concern for the person you're talking to causes you to bring up the name of Jesus, things are going to get a bit dicey. Remember, His name is explosive material.

The Best Offense

If the name of Jesus is so powerful, won't it blow people out of the water? Won't they be offended?

Sometimes the thought of being offensive messengers scares us. Identifying ourselves with Jesus is the litmus test—the divider between those who are His and those who are not. Jesus warned us that if people didn't listen to Him, they wouldn't listen to us (John 15:18–21). Once you show yourself a friend of Jesus, you become an enemy of the world. That's a frightening prospect. After all, you have to live here.

But wait! Why *not* be rejected by the world and accepted by God? Jesus said that if we are ashamed of Him before others, He will be ashamed of us before His Father (Mark 8:38). If people reject you when you come in Jesus' name, they would have rejected Him as well (Luke 10:16).

You may in fact turn out to be an offensive messenger—not because of your style, we hope, but because you are delivering an offensive message. "I know very well how foolish the message of the cross sounds to those who are on the road to destruction. But we who are being saved recognize this message as the very power of God" (1 Corinthians 1:18).

Your mental checklist should be:

- *Am I presenting the gospel in a clear and understandable way?*
- *Am I more concerned about the person I'm talking to than I am about myself?*
- *Am I giving this person enough of God's story that he can make an informed choice?*

If you can answer yes to these questions, you will never have to worry about being an offensive messenger.

Now let's talk about the message itself.

The Straight Story

For most of us, perhaps the most difficult part of sharing our faith, after actually taking the leap and starting, is explaining exactly how to be saved. Nevertheless, telling God's plan of salvation is the most crucial part of witnessing. Here is where we unleash elemental forces and decide eternal destinies.

Don't freak out! We're here to help. We've got some fantastic ways of explaining this ultraimportant transaction—ways you can master in a snap, remember with ease, and deliver like a pro.

Think back to the times you have talked about your faith. Did you leave out any major points? Did you feel frustrated that you didn't know how to explain exactly how to become a Christian? Don't be disappointed in yourself; but don't be satisfied, either. You're supposed to be prepared with an answer (1 Peter 3:15, NIV).

Happily, over the years, some left-brained Christians have come up with a few great ways to remember the plan of salvation—The Four Spiritual Laws, the Roman Road, Steps to Peace with God, and others. They're all good. We'll describe three: The ABCs, the Bridge, and One-Verse Evangelism. We'll also talk about those controversial evangelistic tracts.

After you become familiar with these methods, you can pick and choose the approach or combination of approaches you think will be most effective in a particular situation. Your conversation will be different every time and most likely so will the way you explain God's plan. We hope that as you study these techniques, they'll become second nature to you and that you will have no problem clearly explaining the faith that was "once for all handed down to the saints" (Jude 3, NASB).

Coming to God Is As Easy As ABC

A= Admit you have a problem.
B= Believe Jesus is the Son of God.
C= Confess it to someone.

Admit that you've missed the mark on what God wants for you. You've failed to meet the standard God set for your life (Romans 3:23). In order to receive Christ as your personal Savior, you must admit you have a problem. You also have to be willing to make a 180-

degree turn and start going in the opposite direction. This is called repentance, the starting point of salvation.

Believe that Jesus is the Son of God who said, "I am the way, the truth, and the life. No one can come to the Father except through me" (John 14:6). He didn't say He was one way among many; He said He was *the* way. Through our sins we wrong God and separate ourselves from Him. When a wrong has been committed, justice must be served. God came to earth in the form of a man, Jesus of Nazareth, to give His life to satisfy God's demand for justice and reconcile us to God (Romans 5:8).

Confess your need for God. First, confess to God the things you've done that have displeased Him. Confess that you've lived your life according to your plan, not according to His. Then ask Him to take over. Give Jesus the reins of your life. Finally, confess to another person that you've asked Jesus to take control of your life, that you believe God raised Him from the dead for you, and that you're going to spend eternity in heaven with Him (Romans 10:9). Jesus said that if we will confess Him before others, He will confess us before His Father.

By remembering the ABCs—admit, believe, and confess—you can be certain that you've covered the plan of salvation. It's a simple technique that has been used in countless witnessing sessions, altar calls, and in just about every sermon Billy Graham has ever preached. It's a simple and basic way to talk about Jesus without freaking out.

Jesus Is the Bridge

"The Bridge" originally came from the Navigators. It is now available through NavPress, which has given us permission to adapt it for use here. Over the years we've expanded it for our class. It's a concise way to explain the gospel by using just Scripture verses.[1]

The title comes from man's dilemma: As much as man desires to reach out to God or to please Him, he can't do it on his own. God is aware of the problem, and He has a solution. Knowing that Satan tries to pull us away, God sent Jesus to earth to bridge the gap between God and us so that we are no longer separated. All we have to do is confess our imperfection and need for God, believe who Jesus is, and accept Him into our lives. That's it!

Now we'll explain it in more detail, showing how Bible verses can tell this story better than we ever could in our own words. In our classes, we have each person memorize the verses that make up the Bridge. That way, they're prepared to explain it at any time. You can do the same!

Man has a problem.

O─ Key verses: Romans 3:23; Romans 6:23; Hebrews 9:27

God loves you and has a wonderful plan for your life. He wants you to experience peace and joy. He is not out to destroy you or keep you from having fun. He cares about your personal well-being. He created you and knew you before the beginning of time. That's what the Bible says.

If God planned for us to have peace and abundant life, why are most people miserable? Well, when God created us, He gave us a free will. He did not make us like robots, programmed to obey and love Him no matter what. He gave us an ability to choose. It was in our choice that we blew it. We chose to disobey, walk away from God, and go our own way, and our choice separated us from God. Does this make sense to you?

The bottom line is that man has a problem. We are sinful and separated from God. That is why we feel empty inside. The Bible shows us in Romans (in the New Testament) that all have sinned and failed God (Romans 3:23). We've fallen short of His ideal. The price of our sin is death, a permanent physical and spiritual separation from the eternal God. Further, the Bible tells us that we have only one life to live and one death. Then God will judge the life we chose to live (Hebrews 9:27).

In the Old Testament of the Bible, the prophet Isaiah says that our failures have separated us from God. Our blatant rebellion has hidden His face from us so that He does not hear us. Our sin has caused a great chasm between God and us. Through the centuries many people have tried to close this gap with good efforts, good morals, religion, philosophy, charity, meditation, attempted perfection, and so on. No matter what they have tried, they have always come up short. No one has ever found true peace through human effort.

If all this is true, how can we have a relationship with God? How can we approach Him? And how do we deal with the huge gap that separates us from Him?

Jesus is the answer.

⊙━ Key verses: Isaiah 59:2; Ephesians 2:8–9, (NIV).

The Bible tells us that Jesus Christ is the only way to bridge the gap between sinful, rebellious man and the one Holy God. God's only answer for man's problem is Jesus.

Jesus died a real, physical death on the cross to pay the price for our sins. Three days later, He physically rose from the dead. That's why we celebrate Easter. Jesus is a free gift to us, and we have the choice to accept or reject Him. The Bible says that we have been saved by grace, through faith. "It is the gift of God—not by works, so that no one can boast" (Ephesians 2:8–9, NIV). By accepting Jesus you can know and experience God's love personally. And you can discover His personal plan for your life.

Jesus is God's solution.

⊙━ Key verses: John 10:10; John 3:16; John 5:24

Jesus said, "I assure you, those who listen to my message and believe in God who sent me have eternal life. They will never be condemned for their sins, but they have already passed from death into

Jesus is the Bridge

God's Provision

I and the Father are one. (John 10:30)

But God demonstrates his love for us in this: While we were still sinners, Christ died for us. (Romans 5:8)

Jesus answered, "I am the way and the truth and life. No one comes to the Father except through me." (John 14:6)

For this reason the Jews tried all the harder to kill him; not only was he breaking the Sabbath, but he was even calling God his own Father, making himself equal with God. (John 5:18)

God's Solution

The thief comes only to steal and kill and destroy; I have come that they may have life, and have it to the full. (John 10:10)

For God so loved the world that he gave his one and only Son, that whoever believes in him shall not perish but have eternal life. (John 3:16)

I tell you the truth, whoever hears my word and believes him who sent me has eternal life and will not be condemned; he has crossed over from death to life. (John 5:24)

Man's Response

Yet to all who received him, to those who believed in his name, he gave the right to become children of God. (John 1:12)

Here I am, I stand at the door and knock. If anyone hears my voice and opens the door, I will go in and eat with him, and he with me. (Revelation 3:20)

That if you confess with your mouth, "Jesus is Lord," and believe in your heart that God raised him from the dead, you will be saved. (Romans 10:9)

I pray that you be active in sharing your faith, so that you will have a full understanding of every good thing we have in Christ. (Philemon 6)

- Religion
- Good Works
- Being Good

For it is by grace you have been saved through faith—and this is not from yourselves, it is a gift of God—not by works, so that no one can boast. (Ephesians 2:8–9)

Man's Problem

For all have sinned and fallen short of the glory of God. (Romans 3:23)

For the wages of sin is death, but the free gift of God is eternal life through Jesus Christ our Lord. (Romans 6:23)

Just as a man is destined to die once, and after that to face judgment. (Hebrews 9:27)

But your iniquities have separated you from your God; your sins have hidden his face from you, so that he will not hear. (Isaiah 59:2)

God's Assurance

I write these things to you who believe in the name of the Son of God so that you may know that you have eternal life. (1 John 5:13)

My sheep listen to my voice; I know them, and they follow me. I give them eternal life, and they shall never perish; no one can snatch them out of my hand. (John 10:27–28)

Keep your lives free from the love of money and be content with what you have, because God has said, "Never will I leave you; never will I forsake you." (Hebrews 13:5) life" (John 5:24). Jesus tells us that the devil, not God, comes to kill, steal, and destroy, but that He came that we might have life and have it more abundantly (John 10:10).

Man has a response.

O—⊶ Key verses: John 1:12; Revelation 3:20; Romans 10:9

It's not enough to know these things intellectually. Before you can experience God's love and plan for your life, you must personally receive Jesus Christ as Savior and Lord. This is a choice each individual makes for himself. Jesus will come into your life only by personal invitation.

There is a wonderful promise in the Bible: "Look! Here I stand at the door and knock. If you hear me calling and open the door, I will come in, and we will share a meal as friends" (Revelation 3:20). He's waiting for you to invite Him in.

God shows the way.

O—⊶ Key verses: John 10:30; Romans 5:8; John 14:6

You can receive this great gift through prayer. Prayer is simply talking to God. God knows what's in your heart, and He's more concerned about that than He is with the words you use to express it.

Here is an example of a prayer you can pray if you'd like to ask Jesus Christ to come into your life:

> Lord Jesus, I need You. Thank You for dying on the cross for me. I open the door of my life and receive You as my Savior and Lord. Please forgive my sins, my failures, and my shortcomings. And thank You for giving me eternal life. Come take over the driver's seat of my life. Make me the kind of person You want me to be. Amen.

If this prayer expresses the desire of your heart, please repeat it to God right now and accept His gift of eternal life.

God gives us His assurance.

⊙— Key verses: 1 John 5:11–13; Hebrews 13:5; John 10:27–28
If you ask Jesus into your life, you have the assurance of God's written Word that He has indeed come into your life:

> And this is what God has testified: He has given us eternal life, and
> this life is in his Son. So whoever has God's Son has life; whoever
> does not have his Son does not have life.
> I write this to you who believe in the Son of God, so
> that you may know you have eternal life.
>
> 1 JOHN 5:11–13

Hebrews 13:5 tells us "I will never fail you. I will never forsake you." If we ask Him to come into our lives, He comes to stay!

In summary, God's plan of salvation consists of a few simple steps of faith. First, admit that you are a sinner and that you need God. Second, be willing to turn away from your wrongdoing through repentance. Third, believe that Jesus Christ died for you personally on the cross and rose from the grave to conquer death. Fourth, through prayer, invite Jesus Christ to come into your life through the Holy Spirit, and receive Him as Lord and Savior.

Welcome to a new, exciting, and eternal life!

One-Verse Evangelism

What if you could explain the entire plan of salvation using only one verse from the Bible—and a familiar verse at that? Here it is. We think you're going to like it.[2]

134

For the wages of sin is death, but the gift of God is eternal life in Jesus Christ our Lord (Romans 6:23)

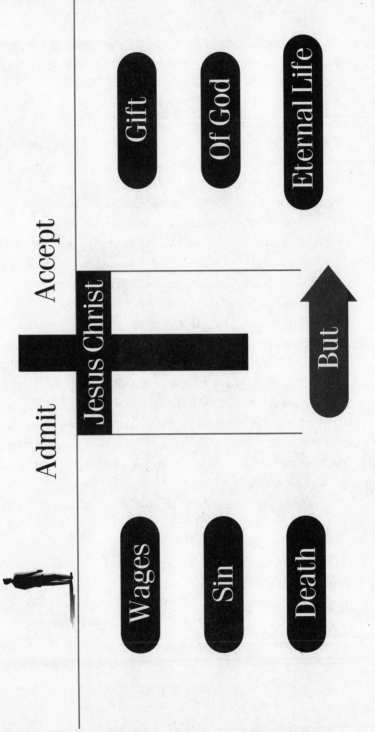

You'll need a pen and paper (or lipstick and napkin). The diagram you're going to draw is very similar to the Bridge, but you may find the process simpler.

Begin by writing your one verse—Romans 6:23—at the top of the page. Here it is in the New International Version: "For the wages of sin is death, but the gift of God is eternal life in Christ Jesus our Lord."

Twenty words. Not so tough, huh? Memorizing them is the hardest part of this method. Once you've learned them, you'll just be talking about them one by one.

For the wages of sin is death, but the gift of God is eternal life in Christ Jesus our Lord.
ROMANS 6:23

Now draw your two cliffs, separated by a chasm. In the left cliff, write the word *wages*. Ask the person, "What are wages?" Wages are what you get for work you do, right? It's something that's earned.

Now write the word *sin*. Again, ask, "What is sin?" Sin is missing the mark. It's anything God doesn't like—like disobeying God's commands and not living up to His standards.

Now write *death*. Ask, "What is death?" Death is the end of life, of course, but it's also a separation. Ultimately, death is eternal separation from God. See how you're just going through the verse one word at a time?

So what you earn by disobeying God is eternal separation from Him. Hmm. That sounds bad. Take a minute to talk about this problem of separation. Talk about Adam and Eve if you want to. Talk about man's attempts to get back to God through good deeds, morality, and religiosity. All of them fail utterly. We cannot leap this divide. All our attempts fall short of the glory of God (Romans 3:23).

But there is hope! See that little conjunction there? *But*. Write *but* at the bottom of the pit between the two cliffs. From now on, you'll be contrasting words across the divide.

Now write *gift* inside the right cliff. Ask, "What is a gift?" Do you pay for a gift that's to be given to you? Not usually. A true gift is free. Compare that to *wages*. Which is sweeter to receive: something you earned, or something someone else paid for?

Next, write *God* or *of God*. Ask, "What is God like?" There is no sin in God. In fact, He cannot tolerate sin in His presence. That's how we got into this mess in the first place—Adam and Eve sinned, and so have we.

Now write *eternal life*. What does that mean? Life everlasting. Eternity in the presence of God. Compare that with *death,* which is eternal separation from God.

Let's review: What you earn from your disobedience to God is eternal death, but what you freely receive from God is eternal life with Him. Sounds wonderful, doesn't it? Is there a catch? Let's look at the rest of the verse.

"In Christ Jesus our Lord." Draw a cross bridging the divide. Draw a stick figure on the left side (you can do this at any point). Explain that *in* carries the meaning of *through*. We cross from death to life *through* Jesus Christ—through His finished work on the cross and His resurrection. Draw an arrow from the left side of the bridge to the right. Maybe even cross out the stick figure on the left and draw him on the right.

Two more words to write and you're done: *admit* and *accept*. Write *admit* on the left side of the bridge and *accept* on the right (another version uses *confess* and *surrender*—it's your choice).

Say something like, "To get from this place of sin and death to that place of life in God, you've got to go through Jesus Christ. You do that by doing two things: admitting you are a sinner—that you've done things that have offended God and that your efforts to reach Him have failed—and accepting His free gift of forgiveness and life. You admit you need Him, and then you accept Him into your life as Lord and Savior."

Then comes the fun part: "Does that sound like something you'd like to do right now?" If he agrees, you get the great joy of leading that person in a prayer of salvation.

One More Verse; Same Chorus

As a bonus, here's another way to get into the entire plan of salvation. In this case you use only one brief passage of Scripture. When someone asks what it is that God really wants from us, you can say the same thing Jesus said. When the people asked Him, "'What does God want us to do?' Jesus told them, 'This is what God wants you to do: Believe in the one he has sent'" (John 6:28–29).

This is what God wants you to do: Believe in the one he has sent.
JOHN 6:28–29

It's very simply stated and straight to the point. You believe in Jesus and you've done all that God wants you to do. Just explaining that verse allows you the opportunity to lay out the entire plan of salvation to someone.

Those Dreadful Tracts

In every class we've taught on witnessing, we ask, "Who here hates tracts?" Usually about half the class raises their hand. Then we ask, "Who here has become a Christian because of a tract?" At least one or two hands go up every time.

After that visual exercise we strongly encourage the class to stop saying, "I hate tracts" or "The Bridge is so dry," or "The ABCs sound so juvenile." We need to use every means available to share the gospel. Don't ever say you hate tracts. For every ten people who say that, we find one who became a Christian because he read one. God will use an astonishing array of methods to reach out to people. A tract left at an airport or shopping mall can change a life forever: You never know who's going to come across it.

Most often, people who refuse to use tracts have never even tried them. Their perception of tracts as a "Christianese" approach turns them off. Or they have negative feelings about them because they've seen a Christian use them in an offensive or pushy manner.

Remember that God is bigger than any means, method, or material that we use to present His story. We just need to decide what's the most helpful tool for us when we're sharing our faith. If someone has offended us by the way he explained the gospel, we should not confuse *what* he told us with *how* he told us. The messenger can be offensive and the message can be convicting, but the material isn't usually what causes the tension.

Over the years, we've heard about some very creative ways that people have used tracts successfully. We thought you'd like to hear a couple of them.

Flower Power

In the 1970s, Jeff became a Christian while hitchhiking in Southern California. A Vietnam veteran picked him up. Across the front dashboard of his car was an assortment of tracts, and as he drove down the highway, the vet told Jeff about Jesus. When he dropped Jeff off at his destination, he handed him a tract.

Jeff showed no interest and got out of the car as quickly as possible. But when he read the tract later, he realized that he needed Jesus in his life. That same evening he prayed by himself to become a Christian. Jeff now looks forward to the day—on earth or in heaven—when he can thank the man who had the courage to tell a young, disinterested hippie hitchhiker about Jesus.

Now Jeff pastors one of the fastest-growing churches in the

Midwest and heads up a global disaster relief and outreach organization. One lone man armed with a tract has touched the lives of hundreds of thousands of people around the world with the love of Jesus.

The Tract Elf

A TV network executive, who was Jewish, asked Mary to baby-sit his two children. A Jewish believer, Mary had a heart for them and their parents, and they liked her. Every time Mary was there she prayed for an opportunity to talk to them about Jesus. She knew they needed Jesus, even if they didn't.

Mary left tracts specifically designed to reach Jewish people around the house—on the toilet, under the sofa cushions—anywhere they would be found after she left. But she left no explanation of why she was doing it or what they were for, because, frankly, she didn't have the nerve.

After a couple of months, the executive suddenly stopped calling Mary to baby-sit. She assumed it was because the tracts she had left had offended them. Finally one day the man came to her office and told her that he hadn't been calling her because he had hired a full-time nanny. He said they all missed her.

In fact, he said he had been meaning to thank Mary for talking to his kids about their Messiah and leaving the little pamphlets around the house. He and his whole family had found them, read them—and had all come to Christ!

Tract Tips

So, now that you're excited about tracts—right?—let's talk about how to use them. Here are some ways to use tracts effectively:

- *Have your listener follow along as you read the pages in order to keep yourself and him focused on Jesus instead of wandering from the main issue.*

- *Use it as a guide when you're nervous so you don't forget what to say or clam up out of fear. If you've got one in your wallet or purse, even a total brainlock won't prevent you from explaining the plan of salvation.*

- *Talk through the points of the tract, and then let the listener take it with him to reread and use as a guide for saying a prayer of commitment.*

- *Hand it to someone when you don't have time to talk.*

- *Put one in the Bible that you give as a gift.*

- *Include one in a letter when you're explaining your faith.*

- *Always have one in your purse, wallet, back pocket, or glove compartment so that a searching person crossing your path in a divine appointment won't be left uninformed.*

Choose a tract that you find comfortable to use. Then learn how to present it. Pray that the Lord will bring you the people who need to have it. Then watch how God always answers the prayers of the righteous.

But beware: When you have a tract around, God will surely have you use it!

Steps to Peace with God

On the following two pages are a copy of a tract that we find very effective in sharing God's story with people today. It is published by the Billy Graham Association. It's the most attractive and informative tract we've read.

Steps To Peace With God

Since God planned for us to have peace and abundant life right now, why are most people not having this experience?

God's Purpose: Peace and Life

God loves you and wants you to experience peace and life—abundant and eternal.

The Bible Says:

"We have peace with God through our Lord Jesus Christ." Romans 5:1

"For God so loved the world that He gave His only begotten Son, that whoever believes in Him should not perish but have everlasting life." John 3:16

"I have come that they may have life, and that they may have it more abundantly." John 10:10b

---

Our Problem: Separation

God created us in His own image to have an abundant life. He did not make us as robots to automatically love and obey Him, but gave us a will and a freedom of choice.

We chose to disobey God and go our own willful way. We still make this choice today. This results in separation from God.

The Bible Says:

"For all have sinned and fallen short of the Glory of God." Romans 3:23

"For the wages of sin is death, but the gift of God is eternal life in Christ Jesus our Lord." Romans 6:23

Our choice results in separation from God.

People (Sinful)   God (Holy)

Our Attempts

Through the ages, individuals have tried in many ways to bridge this gap—without success.

The Bible Says...

"There is a way that seems right to man, but in the end it leads to death." Proverbs 14:12

"But your iniquities have separated you from God; and your sins have hidden His face from you, so that He will not hear." Isaiah 59:2

There is only one remedy for this problem of separation.

Good Works
Religion
Philosophy
Morality

People (Sinful)   God (Holy)

God's Remedy: The Cross

Jesus Christ is the only answer to this problem. He died on the cross and rose from the grave, paying the penalty for our sin and bridging the gap between God and people.

The Bible Says:

"God is on one side and all the people on the other side, and Christ Jesus, Himself man, is between them to bring them together." 1 Timothy 2:5

"For Christ also has suffered once for sins, the just for the unjust, that He might bring us to God." 1 Peter 3:18a

"But God demonstrates His own love for us in this: While we were still sinners, Christ died for us." Romans 5:8

God has provided the only way... we must make the choice...

Christ

People (Sinful)   God (Holy)

Our Response:
Receive Christ

We must trust Jesus Christ and receive Him by personal invitation.

The Bible Says:

"Behold, I stand at the door and knock. If anyone hears My voice and opens the door, I will come in to him and dine with him, and he with Me." Revelation 3:20

"But as many as received Him, to them He gave the right to become children of God, even to those who believe in His name." John 1:12

"If you confess with your mouth the Lord Jesus and believe in your heart that God raised Him from the dead, you will be saved." Romans 10:9

Are you here...   or here?

Christ

People
*Sin
Rebellion
Separation*

God
*Peace
Forgiveness
Abundant Life
Eternal Life*

Is there any good reason why you cannot receive Jesus Christ right now?

How to receive Christ:

1. Admit your need (I am a sinner).

2. Be willing to turn from your sins (repent).

3. Believe that Jesus Christ died for you on the cross and rose from the grave.

4. Through prayer, invite Jesus Christ to come in and control your life through the Holy Spirit. (Receive Him as Lord and Savior.)

What to Pray:

Dear Lord Jesus,
I know that I am a sinner and need Your forgiveness. I believe that You died for my sins. I want to turn from my sins. I now invite You to come into my heart and life. I want to trust and follow You as Lord and Savior. In Jesus' name. Amen.

_____

Date   Signature

God's Assurance:
His Word

If you prayed this prayer,

The Bible Says...

"For 'whoever calls upon the name of the Lord will be saved.'"
Romans 10:13

Did you sincerely ask Jesus Christ to come into your life? Where is He right now? What has He given you?

"For it is by grace you have been saved, through faith—and this is not from yourselves, it is the gift of God—not by works, so that no one can boast." Ephesians 2:8-9

The Bible Says:

"He who has the Son has life; he who does not have the Son of God does not have life. These things I have written to you who believe in the name of the Son of God, that you may know that you have eternal life, and that you may continue to believe in the name of the Son of God."
1 John 5:12-13, NKJV

Receiving Christ, we are born into God's family through the supernatural work of the Holy Spirit who indwells every believer. This is called regeneration or the "new birth."

This is just the beginning of a wonderful new life in Christ. To deepen this relationship you should:

1. Read your Bible every day to know Christ better.

2. Talk to God in prayer every day.

3. Tell others about Christ.

4. Worship, fellowship, and serve with other Christians in a church where Christ is preached.

5. As Christ's representative in a needy world, demonstrate your new life by your love and concern for others.

God bless you as you do.

It's Time to Pray

Once you have led a person through the plan of salvation, and he understands what God has to offer him and has decided to accept the gift of Jesus, you get the incredible privilege of praying with him.

This can be a scary step, but don't freak out! Suddenly you're embarrassed. You're convinced he wants you to stop talking so he can be alone and think about what you've said. You decide that the time is wrong or the place is inappropriate or the weather is bad and that you should stop while you're ahead.

This is Satan's last-ditch effort. You've done irreparable damage to one of his own, but until that prayer is prayed, it's still anybody's soul.

Some people feel no hesitation at this point whatsoever. They've broken so many barriers, they're not about to stop now! They know they'd better strike while the iron's hot because the enemy is going to do his best to cool everything down if they leave without pressing for a commitment.

Other people sincerely wonder if it would be better to wait. In some cases, it might be. You'll just have to ask God for discernment. But here's a tip: If you're hesitating out of anything that feels like fear, don't stop! Press on.

All you have to do is to ask a simple question: "Does this sound like something you'd like to do?" or "Is there any reason you wouldn't ask Jesus to take over your life right now?" Offer him the opportunity to accept Jesus right then and there. The worst thing he can say is no. The most wonderful thing he can say is yes.

It's a step worth taking—one someone once took for you—so make yourself step out of your comfort zone and ask that last, vitally important question. It all comes down to this: Don't let Satan win a soul just because you chicken out.

Praying with someone may seem like it would be hard, but it usually isn't. At this point, the person trusts you completely. He wants what you have described. Even if you garble the prayer now, you've given him enough truth that he'll know what you mean.

The prayer is important because through it the person publicly confesses his commitment to Jesus. He is confessing with his mouth that Jesus is Lord and believing in his heart that God raised him from the dead (Romans 10:9). When that happens, the Bible says, he will be saved.

Trust us, when you pray with a new believer, it will be one of the most meaningful moments in your life. There is nothing more exciting to us than being a part of someone's decision to become a follower of Jesus. It's the best!

The Sinner's Prayer

There is no one way to pray the prayer of salvation. The sinner's prayer refers simply to what a person says to God when he commits his life to Christ. The Bible doesn't say that Jesus ever led anyone in "the sinner's prayer," so don't feel like there is a special prayer someone has to say to become a full-fledged Christian or make his salvation "take."

A person can merely thank God for revealing Himself to him. Sometimes, that's all he needs to do. If you know what you want the person to acknowledge, ask him to tell God that in prayer. Then don't worry about what he says. There are no magic words. We had a friend who merely thanked Jesus for being with us and listening to our prayers—and his life was forever changed. That acknowledgment was all the Lord needed.

The elements of this prayer are easy to remember because you know what the goal is: to help a person ask Jesus into his life and place Him in charge. We recommend that you lead the person in prayer—you say the prayer first and the person echoes each phrase. Although any prayer will do, here's what a prayer of salvation might sound like:

> *Dear Jesus, I want to know You personally.*
> *I confess my life has disappointed You.*
> *Please forgive me for all the things I've done wrong.*
> *I believe that You died on the cross to pay for my sins,*
> *and that You rose from the dead to give me eternal life.*
> *Please come into my life now, Jesus, and take over for me.*
> *Thank You for making me the kind of person You want me to be.*
> *Now, Jesus, show me what to do next.*
>
> AMEN.

Now You Know What to Do

Now you can step out boldly, knowing that you are you prepared to tell the three stories involved in sharing your faith: their story, your story, and His story.

Every time you share any portion of your faith in Jesus, you are doing God's will. You are sprinkling eternal seeds that will be scattered on the souls of those around you. They will either take root, be washed away, get choked out, or multiply a hundredfold. Only God knows the condition of the ground that seed is falling on. Isn't it wonderful that it's not up to you? The only part you are responsible for is to sow the seed and pray.

Many times we Christians gain the courage to share glimpses of our faith but don't follow through. We tell a bit about our own spiritual journey and ask some questions about the other person, but we don't quite get to what it actually means to become a Christian. We fail to get to the meat of the gospel, chickening out just short of offering the remedy for the fatal condition of mankind. What a shame.

That comes from two things: a lack of information and fear. Now you have the information you need, so there's nothing to be afraid of. Both hindrances are gone. You know how to express the truth of the gospel. You will soon have all the necessary verses memorized. You've got your testimony prepared and some great witnessing techniques at your beck and call. You understand that the listener's response is no reflection on your delivery of the information. Wow! You've gotten through the toughest part. The rest is icing on the cake. Are you ready?

Now for the Don'ts

We had to have some, didn't we?

- *Don't be afraid to say something.*

- *Don't think that time alone with someone is a coincidence.*

- *Don't allow yourself to rationalize away the opportunity.*

- *Don't let the devil get you to freeze up and sit down.*

- *Don't believe that you won't speak well, clearly, or intelligently.*

- *Don't believe that the person won't be interested.*

- *Don't believe that you'll offend him or her.*

- *Don't stop reading this book.*

- *And most importantly, don't freak out!*

1 Adapted from "The Bridge" © 1997. Used by permission of NavPress, Colorado Springs, Col. All rights reserved.

2. One-Verse Evangelism was developed by Pastor Bob Neely of North Richland Hills Baptist Church, Fort Worth, Texas. We use it here with his permission.

CHAPTER EIGHT

A Word to New Believers

He who began a good work in you will carry it
on to completion until the day of Christ Jesus.
PHILIPPIANS 1:6, NIV

Victorya Says: I have a friend, Chris, who is well known in Hollywood. Because she is a Hollywood celebrity, she found it difficult to find a quality guy interested in her instead of her TV persona. She had gone from one heartbreak to another and was getting tired of it all.

She said she had achieved everything she had ever dreamed of, yet she still wasn't happy. How I wished she would try Jesus. But she felt Christianity was for me and not her. I talked to her about God many times, and one time I even walked her through the plan of salvation. But she just wasn't ready. After six years, I was getting discouraged. But I kept praying.

Then after Chris went through another devastating breakup, a girlfriend invited her to a Christian concert just to get her out of the house. Chris called to let me know she was going to the concert because she knew I'd be thrilled—and I was. The news that followed was even more exciting. Afterwards, she called me to announce that at the concert she had accepted Jesus Christ as her personal Savior. Finally! God is still in the business of answering prayer.

We've Only Just Begun

By the time you come to this section of the book, you may have been blessed by having your pre-Christian friend accept Jesus as his personal Savior. Congratulations to both of you! The Scriptures tell us that the angels are singing in heaven right now because of you (Luke 15:10). There is nothing more fulfilling than being part of someone's successful journey to Christ.

Finally your friend has accepted Jesus. Now what do you do? Over the years we've noticed that sometimes after a Christian has led someone to the Lord, he feels that his work is done. The harvest is in! It's time to rejoice and relax. But really, this new believer is more at a beginning than an end. Do you just turn him over to his own devices? No! He's a tiny baby in the faith. He needs parents; he needs care; he needs instruction; he needs food.

Are you responsible for him spiritually? No. You can't give him all that, so don't try. Would it be appropriate to help guide him forward in his walk with God? Yes. You need to make sure he's in a position to receive everything he needs to grow in his new faith. And the very first thing he needs is to know he is saved—once and for all.[1]

Don't Leave Me!

There is a pattern that, although it does not apply universally, seems to be typical for a lot of new Christians. When a person becomes a Christian, he experiences a surge of God's Holy Spirit in his life. He starts seeing things differently. He gets hungry for the Bible and begins to read it voraciously. He joins a Bible study, tells everyone he knows

150

what he has learned, and if the other people around him don't do the same, feels led to make it clear what they're missing. The new believer is on fire for the Lord and enjoying every moment of it.

Then comes a day when the fire dies down. Having shown him the potential of his faith, God steps back to let the new believer learn to walk on his own two feet. God is always near, lovingly watching out for him, but giving him a chance to grow up and learn to be more independent. What he needs is a sustainable fire, not a wildfire.

The believer, however, panics and interprets this as God pulling away and leaving him alone again, as he was before his conversion. He starts to doubt God's personal involvement in his life and wonders what this Christianity thing is really all about. He sometimes goes through a dark time of questioning and confusion.

If he intensifies his study of God's Word, the new believer will move out of this valley onto a plateau of a more solid faith. He starts to understand that his relationship with the Lord is deeper and subtler than what he first experienced. He begins to accept God's quiet guidance and care and comes to understand that God's promises and the Holy Spirit's power are what builds his faith. These facts, he realizes, must come before feelings in his relationship with his Lord.

This is a healthy journey. However, what sometimes happens is that the person does not learn these truths. If he doesn't, he can initiate a destructive cycle in his Christian walk. If he keeps walking in circles, his spiritual fire can completely die out.

In *Grace Walk* author Steve McVey says, "I lived many years of my Christian life trapped in what I call the motivation-condemnation-rededication cycle."[2] He would determine to live a good Christian life, not live up to his expectation of what that was, fall into condemnation and defeat, and then, confessing "spiritual slothfulness," rededicate his life to God. This went on for years until he became completely discouraged.

151

I would ask God to help me be more consistent. I would promise to read my Bible more, pray more, win more souls, whatever I thought it took to get back on course. I resolved to try harder than ever to live for God. Yet no matter how hard I tried, I never experienced real peace about my Christian life.[3]

Years later, after he had been totally broken before the Lord, Steve came to understand that "Christianity isn't built around performance, but is centered on the person of Jesus Christ.... Christianity is not rules and routine, but a relationship! The key to enjoying success as a Christian is not strenuous work, but spiritual rest."[4]

Unless new Christians know that they are eternally secure, they can easily fall into this same pattern of committing their lives to God over and over again in an exhausting, endless cycle. This leads to a life of mediocrity and frustration, which is not at all what God intends for His children.

Because our salvation is about a relationship with Jesus that is nurtured in spiritual rest, we must pass on the good news that once we ask Jesus to have a relationship with us, we have it for life. It is something we must make clear to a new believer.

After you have led someone to Christ, warn him about this pitfall and help him choose the first path rather than the second. Explain that assurance of faith means that God will never leave you. Eternal security means that you know that you are saved regardless of your feelings, your circumstances, or your level of faith. It helps to give a new believer a Bible and write the date of his salvation in it as a lifelong reminder of God's commitment.

Jesus tells us that just as a shepherd protects his sheep from harm, He will always protect each one of His children, whom He knows by name. Even when we go through difficult times on earth, Jesus is always with us, so there is no reason to be afraid. He assures us that if we choose to follow Him, once and for all, He will give us everlasting safety.

We have our class members memorize three Scriptures to remind them of the assurance of their salvation and to enable them to tell others about that truth.

Eternal Security Scripture #1:

[Jesus said:] My sheep recognize my voice; I know them, and they follow me. I give them eternal life, and they will never perish. No one will snatch them away from me. (John 10:27–28)

Eternal Security Scripture #2:

Stay away from the love of money; be satisfied with what you have. For God has said, "I will never fail you. I will never forsake you." (Hebrews 13:5)

Eternal Security Scripture #3

I write this to you who believe in the Son of God, so that you may know you have eternal life. (1 John 5:13)

Many times in the Old and New Testaments, God proclaims His unconditional love for us. That's sometimes a tough concept to grasp because human love is always to some degree conditional. God wants the best for you, has a plan for you, and knows what you need. He will *never* leave you or turn away from you. You don't have to work for it. You don't have to ask Him to prove it to you. The bottom line is He said it, so it's true.

So your friend has become a Christian and understands that he is now a child of God, a new creature forever, no matter what. Hallelujah! Now he gets to begin the exciting job of developing a relationship with Jesus.

Holy Spirit Maid Service

A new Christian needs to understand that once saved, he's secure but not "done." In fact he has just started. Now begins the process of developing an intimate relationship with his Savior.

If the new believer is a friend, colleague, or relative, we encourage you to stay involved and help guide him in his new Christian life, especially in the beginning. It would be best to bring him to church with you and commit to disciple him yourself. Unfortunately, that's not always possible. If the person was a stranger, you may not see him regularly. In this case, it is important that you point him in the right direction during your encounter. Remember, this is a whole new world to this new Christian. He's like a bushman in Paris. Be a friend and help him get to where he needs to go.

You might get some good booklets on spiritual growth and keep them on hand. Many local churches offer them, and they often have the church address and telephone number printed on the back. Try to recommend a local church for him to get plugged in to, or in some way offer a tangible next step to keep him moving forward in his new faith.

Our spiritual lives are like our houses: We don't notice the dust when they are cluttered and messy. Why? Because the mess is covering up the dust. As we straighten things up and put away the clutter, we start seeing the dust again. When all the stuff is put away, we start the deep cleaning. As a new Christian starts to clean up his life, God will begin to reveal the sins that need to be dealt with.

God is merciful: He doesn't overwhelm us. He cleans one room thoroughly, then moves on to the next. Spiritual growth is a lifelong process of seeking God and allowing Him to change one thing at a time in us. It's a thrilling process that comes only through an intimate relationship with Jesus.

This is helpful for a new believer to know so that he doesn't become frustrated if his life doesn't change overnight or if a certain struggle doesn't immediately disappear. All he needs to do is to pursue a personal relationship with God, keep saying yes to the prompting of the Holy Spirit, and allow Jesus to deal with the clutter He reveals.

Dust builds up. It seems that we dust on Monday and by Tuesday everything is dusty again. This happens in our spiritual lives as well. We get cleaned up and then run out and get dirty all over again.

Here are five steps a new believer should take to keep the spiritual dust from building up: Talk to Jesus often, read the Bible daily, find a church home, get baptized, and talk about Jesus to others.

Five Steps for the New Believer

1. Talk to Jesus often.

Just as we need to spend time with family and friends to build intimate relationships with them, so we need to spend time in prayer to develop an intimate relationship with God. We cannot sustain spiritual life for long without it.

For many, understanding prayer as God's gift to us may be a new concept. Prayer is the privilege of speaking directly to the God of the universe anytime, anywhere, for free. Many of us have grown up thinking of God as distant and unreachable. Jesus said differently:

> *Keep on asking, and you will be given what you ask for.*
> *Keep on looking, and you will find.*
> *Keep on knocking, and the door will be opened.*
> *For everyone who asks, receives.*
> *Everyone who seeks, finds.*
> *And the door is opened to everyone who knocks.*
> MATTHEW 7:7–8

155

We have an open invitation to speak to God about anything. We can talk to Him when we are happy or sad, excited or angry, confused or scared. And He listens. Many times we may feel too inadequate to approach God, but He urges us to come to Him just as we are. "If you need wisdom—if you want to know what God wants you to do—ask him, and he will gladly tell you. He will not resent your asking" (James 1:5).

In *Prayer: Finding the Heart's True Home*, Richard J. Foster says:

We all come to prayer with a tangled web of motives— altruistic and selfish, merciful and hateful, loving and bitter.... God is big enough to receive us with all our mixture. We do not have to be bright, or pure, or filled with faith, or anything. That is what grace means; and not only are we saved by grace, we live by it as well.[5]

How do we pray or what should we pray for? Jesus specifically answers this question:

Pray like this: Our Father in heaven, may your name be honored.
May your kingdom come soon.
May your will be done here on earth, just as it is in heaven.
Give us our food for today, and forgive us our sins,
just as we have forgiven those who have sinned against us.
And don't let us yield to temptation, but deliver us from the evil one.
MATTHEW 6:9–13

Begin by praising God, recognizing Him for who He is. Then thank Him for the blessings in your life. If there is one habit that will bring happiness to your life, it's thanking God for all the good in your life each and every day! Confess your sins and failures. Then ask God to reveal His will for your life, make your requests known to Him, and pray for others. Finally, ask Him to help you live a holy life, pleasing and acceptable to Him.

> *And we can be confident that he will listen to us*
> *whenever we ask him for anything in line with his will.*
> *And if we know he is listening when we make our requests, we*
> *can be sure that he will give us what we ask for.*
> 1 JOHN 5:14–15

The first thing to tell a new believer to do is to pray. Prayer is to our spirit what water is to our bodies. The second thing to tell him to do is to read the Bible.

2. *Read the Bible daily.*

We can fall in love with someone and believe that we've met the most perfect person in the world. But if we don't develop a relationship with that special person, the love will eventually fade away.

That's the same with Jesus. We have to spend time with Him if we want to get to know Him. We do this not only through prayer, but also by reading the Bible, which reveals Him to us. Only when we know who our true love really is will we experience the depth of His love for us.

As more mature believers, we know that this makes total sense. However, it can be difficult to communicate to a new believer, particularly if he does not have any healthy intimate relationships to draw on as a model in building one with God. One of the reasons why so many of us live defeated or mediocre Christian lives is because we don't know how to develop a meaningful rich relationship with anyone—let alone God.

We all begin our relationship with Jesus by reading His love story. He didn't assume that we would just figure it all out. He laid it out in black and white so that we could all learn about His unconditional love and have the same opportunity for intimacy with Him. Therefore, we have to teach a new believer to read the Bible.

Make sure that the new believer has a Bible and that the translation is suitable for him. (See "So Many Translations!" on page 202.) Help him become familiar with it. Open it up to the table of contents and talk about the main divisions. Some Bibles have cross-references, a concordance, maps, and other helpful features. Explain how to use those and how to get around in both Testaments. In particular, show him how to find John's Gospel. You're handing him a power tool— take some time to show him how it works.

Encourage the new believer to read it often. We need daily Bible reading for spiritual growth just as we need food every day to nourish our physical bodies. Christians cannot survive spiritually for long without both Bible reading and prayer.

3. Find a church home.

It is very important to develop relationships with other Christians. No Christian is an island; we all need a support system. The best way to have this, and the way God designed it, is to join a local church.

A recent study showed that those who go to church regularly with their families are more stable in their personal and business lives, have stronger marriages, are less likely to abuse alcohol or drugs, and even live longer. Encourage the new Christian to visit several churches in his area until he finds one where he enjoys the people and where the teaching is straight from the Bible.

Also recommend that he get involved in an adult Sunday school class or small group at the church. That's the best way to build lasting relationships, especially in large churches where merely attending a service once a week offers little opportunity for interaction with other believers. The small group setting is where real growth happens. Our Sunday school classes have carried us through a lot.

4. Get baptized.

Baptism is an important component of a new Christian's life. We do not believe there is anything magical about the baptismal waters: It doesn't affect your eternal security one way or the other. We believe it is a symbol of what has happened to the new believer. He should think of it as an external picture of an internal reality. His old life has been buried; he rises up to a new life. Jesus has washed away his sin and granted him a fresh start with Him.

Baptism is something a believer does to identify himself with his Lord. Jesus allowed Himself to be baptized, and today Christians still follow His example. Encourage the new believer to demonstrate his allegiance to Christ through this simple act of obedience.

5. Talk about Jesus without freaking out.

Remember when you met the boy or girl of your dreams? Didn't you talk about him or her to everyone you knew? Or remember your baby's first steps? Didn't you brag about your prodigy to anyone who would listen?

We need to tell new believers that they should have this same passion for talking about Jesus. They should be shouting the Good News from the rooftops!

You are the light of the world—like a city on a mountain,
glowing in the night for all to see.
Don't hide your light under a basket!
Instead, put it on a stand and let it shine for all.
In the same way, let your good deeds shine out for all to see, so
that everyone will praise your heavenly Father.
MATTHEW 5:14–16

Instill that passion into your new Christian friends. If they give you the excuse that they're not knowledgeable enough, hand them this book!

Life after Coming to Christ: Is It Perfect?

New Christians sometimes imagine that their lives will henceforth be perfect. They expect problems to go away immediately and forever and nothing but bliss to follow. But make no mistake about it— there will be trials. Life happens!

Having been pushed aside and defeated, Satan sometimes retaliates. He'll bring a few things down on the new believer's head as a final jab (just as the Iraqis set oil fields aflame when they fled Kuwait) or try to make the new believer think he's made a mistake. Tell your friend not to fall for that.

Although God promises us joy, fulfillment, and peace, He does not wave a magic wand to make all our problems disappear. What He does is promise to be with us, teach us, lead us, and show us how to handle the things that come. He most often doesn't change the situation the believer is in; instead He uses the situation to change the believer—to develop character or increase dependence on Him. He never gives us more than we can handle (1 Corinthians 10:13), and He's given us a manual on how to run the race to victory.

Remember that in a race everyone runs, but|
only one person gets the prize.
You also must run in such a way that you will win.
All athletes practice strict self-control.
They do it to win a prize that will fade away, but
we do it for an eternal prize.
So I run straight to the goal with purpose in every step.
I am not like a boxer who misses his punches.

160

I discipline my body like an athlete, training it to do what it should.
Otherwise, I fear that after preaching to others
I myself might be disqualified.
1 CORINTHIANS 9:24–27

Author and speaker Norman Vincent Peale said, "God gives us gifts wrapped up in problems." As we seek to solve each new problem, we need to seek God's guidance and discover what gift He is giving us in His solution. We love hearing this perspective. Now we can look at each problem as a challenge to find the gift inside. How wonderful it would be for a new Christian to learn this lesson early in his journey.

> *"If you cease to have problems, check your pulse."*
> NORMAN VINCENT PEALE

Peale also said, "If you cease to have problems, check your pulse." As long as we live, we will encounter trials and troubles. A new Christian needs to know that the Holy Spirit is inside him, helping him through them.

In addition to trials and troubles, a new believer will continue to be tempted to sin. The devil is not exactly thrilled that there is a new member in the family of God. In fact he'll do as much as he can to discourage, deceive, and distract.[6] But Jesus is faithful to be there beside us. This is God's absolute promise!

But remember that the temptations that come into your life
are no different from what others experience.
And God is faithful. He will keep the temptation from becoming
so strong that you can't stand up against it.
When you are tempted, he will show you a way out
so that you will not give in to it.
1 CORINTHIANS 10:13

We always have a choice when temptations come. We can either choose the right or the wrong response. As a new Christian grows stronger in his spiritual life, he will begin to make the right choices more and more often until it becomes his nature to do it consistently.

But life will never be perfect and won't stay easy for long. Remind new believers that God causes everything to work together for the good of those who love Him and are called according to His purpose (Romans 8:28) and that the God who began a good work in him will see it faithfully through to completion (Philippians 1:6). God's promises are what we must keep in our daily thoughts and actions. If nothing else, remind a new believer of this promise:

> *I am convinced that nothing can ever separate us from his love.*
> *Death can't, and life can't.*
> *The angels can't, and the demons can't.*
> *Our fears for today, our worries about tomorrow, and*
> *even the powers of hell can't keep God's love away.*
> ROMANS 8:38

What a privilege it is to get to speak these words to a new believer!

1. Dr. Bill Bright is an expert on how you can be sure you're a Christian. He has written a number of clear and simple books and pamphlets on this topic. See the recommended reading list in appendix A.

2. Steve McVey, *Grace Walk* (Eugene, Ore.: Harvest House Publishers, 1995), 17.

3. Ibid.

4. Ibid.

5. Richard J. Foster, *Prayer: Finding the Heart's True Home* (San Francisco: HarperSanFrancisco, 1992), 8.

6. C. S. Lewis gives a vivid description of how the devil works in his brilliant short novel, *The Screwtape Letters.*

PART III

No Mission's Impossible

CHAPTER NINE

Tough Nuts to Crack

"Father, forgive these people,
because they don't know what they are doing."
LUKE 23:34

Karen Says: Jim and I attended a cast and crew party of a film for which Jim had written the score. At one point, a loud conversation caught our attention. We quickly eavesdropped on a circle of six men who were talking very negatively about a religious cult. It wasn't long before the conversation shifted to a discussion about Christianity, and the negativity escalated.

We couldn't stand it any longer. Jim poked through a slight gap in the circle as I found my own opening. We slipped in just in time to hear the men agreeing that Christianity was a sham, a scam, and a manipulative ploy by Paul to control the world. That was our cue.

Jim began with a joke—always a great way to start. Then he brought in some apologetics. They were intrigued that an obviously intelligent person could actually believe such things. After a good presentation of the archaeological, historical, and scientific evidence that Jesus is God, Jim stopped for a breath. Two of the men had obviously decided that he was talking rubbish, and they walked away. The other four stayed.

I began a conversation with one of them, Robert, who was intrigued enough to stick around. As we bounced our beliefs back and forth, it became clear that Robert was a hurting, bitter man. His seething hatred for any belief system that included Jesus raised the decibel level of our discussion. At one point I saw that our cluster had shrunk to Robert, one of his friends, Jim, and me. (Was it something we said?)

It wasn't long before our conversation turned into a debate. By then Robert and I were alone and speaking louder than ever. The other guests were watching, though they pretended not to notice. I saw the party's host, the film director, looking very distressed, and it occurred to me that I might have gone too far.

I made a joke about us being thrown out of the party, and Robert kidded that he wasn't going to stop until I realized I was wrong. I told him that would never happen, so we'd better stop now before someone thought we were going to get in a fistfight. Though Robert and I were quite passionate about our own beliefs, we laughed, and it was clear we were both really enjoying the debate. I thanked him for the stimulating conversation and walked away.

Then I saw Robert's wife go straight to him and begin talking heatedly. I was heading toward the house to find Jim when Robert came back toward me. He began apologizing for coming on so strong. I said I was fine and that I was actually going to find his wife to apologize for beating up on her husband. I gave him a big hug, and we decided to walk up to our host and show him that we were still friends.

We went around the party with our arms around each other to show the other guests that we didn't hate each other. By the end of the evening we were buddies, and our debate had become a topic of very interesting conversation.

9

Nutcracking

How do you talk to people who don't think they need Jesus? Atheists, the wealthy, Gen-Xers, New-Agers, cult members, Jewish people, unsaved church members, and those in your own family can all be tough nuts to crack. The reasons you will have trouble speaking to them about Jesus will differ: they may be hostile, apathetic, intolerantly tolerant, bound in cults or culture, or just too close to you. Whatever the reason, there seem to be no chinks in their armor. You know they're in terrible danger without Christ, but they don't know, and they don't want to. It's hard to answer questions no one is asking.

Isn't it strange? Christians have a long list of excuses for not talking about Jesus, and non-Christians have a long list of reasons for not listening. Behind the pretexts of both lies a fear that testifies to the awesome importance of Jesus Christ.

In chapters 2 and 3, we talked about getting past the obstacles to witnessing that Christians find in themselves. In this chapter, we'll talk about the walls nonbelievers put up to keep from being witnessed to, why they put them up, and how to get past them.

Handling Hostility

How do you act when you feel vulnerable, inadequate, or inferior? Some people react in anger, as Robert did at that party. Picture a cornered mountain lion. It knows it is in terrible danger and that its only hope is to launch a stunning attack that will surprise the pursuer and give it a chance to get away. People hostile to Christianity will sometimes launch similar attacks.

The Convicted

Here's a crucial insight into these people: They are hostile because they are convicted. If God has truly created man in His image

(Genesis 1:27), that truth must be planted somewhere deep in the soul of every person. All people struggle with it if they don't embrace God for who He is. Romans says:

> *From the time the world was created, people have*
> *seen the earth and sky and all that God made.*
> *They can clearly see his invisible qualities—*
> *his eternal power and divine nature.*
> *So they have no excuse whatsoever for not knowing God.*
> ROMANS 1:20

The truth causes chaos in the hearts of nonbelievers. Some get so numb they cease to notice; but those who know there must be some truth to this Jesus stuff, but still reject Him, tend to get hostile at the mere mention of His name.

That's the power of conviction. It's what happens when we come unexpectedly into the presence of God. His light reveals our deepest failures. All our camouflage is ripped away. We feel naked, exposed. Now who's freaking out? No wonder some people don't like us to talk about Jesus.

Think about it. You've built your life on the assumption that Jesus is not important, but someone tells you that He's of supreme importance—and part of you wonders if it might be true. Wouldn't that make you angry? Think about everything you'd have to change and give up. You might have to stop sleeping with your girlfriend or boyfriend, admit you've been wrong, or worse, step down off the throne of your life and submit to Someone. No, the price is too high. Your only out is to defend your choices by shouting the person down.

People under conviction often feel they must prove they are just as good or better than other people, especially "born-againers," who they think are totally out to lunch. They take the feeling of convic-

168

tion that has come from God, project it onto you, and accuse you of judging them. They'll call you a narrow-minded, hypocritical finger-pointer. "Who died and made you God?" they'll ask. They're like the person who cuts you off on the freeway, then when you honk to let him know you're there, salutes you with a raised finger.

Wow! Did I step on your last nerve, or what?

The Hurt

Then again, someone may be hostile to you because a person who symbolized religion or God has wronged him. He's still suffering from those wounds, so he'll take any chance he can get to lash out at Christianity. Since he can't take it out on God, he turns on those who represent Him. We know many people who have been hurt "in the name of the Lord."

The Insecure

Hostility is also a common response from those who are unsure of their beliefs. They get nervous when they try to defend their world-view because they don't really have one—not one that makes sense, anyway. They won't even let themselves look too deeply, so they're certainly not going to let you. As a friend of ours says, there is nothing stronger than a weak person defending his weakness.

The Anti-Theist

What about hostile people who don't believe there is a God? It's crucial to understand what an atheist is before trying to figure out how to respond to one. We believe that after you study the definition, you'll be better able to stand firm in your commitment to God when talking with an atheist.

Ravi Zacharias, in his book *Can Man Live Without God?* defines atheism this way:

The atheist, often better described as an anti-theist, attempts to build his or her own life in the belief that there is no God and that there are no supernatural entities.... Atheism contradicts belief in God with a positive affirmation of matter as ultimate reality.[1]

Anti-theists question the whole enchilada: God, eternal life, sin, and hell. They believe that these things don't exist, but they can't empirically prove their nonexistence. Atheists also deny that there is absolute truth, absolute justice, or absolute anything else. Unlike agnostics, who refuse to accept the evidence of revelation and spiritual experience, anti-theists won't even consider the possibility that something exists beyond the scope of their knowledge, understanding, or experience.

Zacharias comments:

All forms of religion they consider irrational, but in kicking against the unavoidable goads along life's path they bloody themselves both intellectually and socially. I am thoroughly convinced that when the last chapter of humanity is written we will find that the implications of atheism, i.e., living without God, if consistently carried through, will have made life plainly unlivable within the limits of reason or even of common sense.[2]

Considered rationally, the concept of atheism is absurd, and trying to live it out is even more so. Atheism is simply not logical. We think it takes a greater leap of faith to accept atheism than it does to accept Christianity.

In your discussions with anti-theists you must remember that they have usually accepted this worldview because, for some reason, they *need* to believe that God doesn't exist. Perhaps it is in order to deal with the hurt, abuse, or emptiness they've experienced in their lives. Some atheists are furious with God, and their anger has brought them to atheism simply as a way of surviving.

Remember that when you are speaking with anti-theists, but don't get too smug. Yes, many people embrace atheism for poor reasons. But have any of us embraced Christianity for poor reasons? Some come to Christ for the same psychological reasons that drive others to atheism. Is your faith nothing but an acceptance of the verses of the Bible that make you feel good? C. S. Lewis writes:

> Very well then, atheism is too simple. And I will tell you another view that is also too simple. It is the view I call Christianity-and-water, the view which simply says there is a good God in Heaven and everything is all right—leaving out all the difficult and terrible doctrines about sin and hell and the devil, and the redemption. Both these are boys' philosophies. It is no good asking for a simple religion. After all, real things are not simple.[3]

If your idea of Christianity is merely that a loving God wants us all to be happy, you may have the same unfounded faith as an atheist. You won't want to respond to one with shallow remarks about a sweet God. You need to be open about God's mysterious ways and honest about some of your own questions. King Solomon reminded us of the need for balance when he said, "The man who fears God will avoid all extremes (Ecclesiastes 7:18, NIV).

We think the best example of a hostile anti-theist was Madalyn Murray O'Hair. She founded American Atheists, Inc. and for more than thirty years was the self-styled "most hated woman in America." Later in life she said that she had rejected God as a youngster, but her son claims that her hatred for God was actually an extension of her hatred of men:

> Madalyn Murray was mad at men, and she was mad at God, who is male. Rather than confront her conscience, she determined to deny God's existence and refused to accept any moral constraints. She had to destroy all references to God, because if there were a Deity, then He could make demands on her life.[4]

O'Hair was a prime example of someone who experienced a severe spiritual struggle and who, instead of facing the battle within, lashed out at anyone or anything that reminded her of the target of her personal anger.

Keeping the Lid On

How can you respond to someone like Madalyn Murray O'Hair?

When a person—atheist or not—responds with hostility when we talk about Jesus, the first thing we need to do is to remind ourselves that he is in a spiritual battle, even though he doesn't know it. If the name of Jesus did not always cause an emotional reaction, people would talk about Him like they do about whitewater rafting or the ice-cream flavor of the month. But He is powerful, so you can expect a variety of responses when you bring Him up. One of them is hostility.

Know that people who respond to you that way are in bondage to their erroneous beliefs and that they have believed the devil's lie that Christianity will bind them further instead of setting them free. Don't take personally anything a hostile person says. In fact, you should thank the Lord that he is still open enough to the truth to react to it. We're intrigued when we meet a hostile person because we know that he could be very close to embracing the Lord.

If someone becomes hostile when you're talking to him about Jesus, don't be alarmed. He isn't mad at you. It's a compliment, really, because he has essentially identified you with Jesus Christ. As far as he's concerned, he's talking to Jesus Himself, giving Him a piece of his mind.

One thing you can do is simply stop the conversation and walk away because now you know how you should pray for that person. Or you can apologize for making him angry and change the subject. Since it is the opposite of what he expects, your sensitivity can minister to him.

You might ask such a person why he is so angry. Remember the power of the probing question. "Are you mad at me because I believe in God, or are you mad at God?" "Are you angry at God or Jesus or both?" "What do you think gets you upset about talking about Jesus?" "What is it about God that irritates you so?" "Have you always hated God?"

When you ask questions like these, you help the person recognize his feelings of hostility. Most likely, no one has ever challenged him about them. You may help him see the extent—or even the source—of his anger. Once that's out in the open, it may be possible for you to go deeper with him about Jesus. Look for opportunities to tell them that the God they claim doesn't exist loves them very much.

The third approach to a hostile person is to ignore his anger altogether. Just let it bounce off you and talk about your personal experience with Jesus—how He always comes through and supplies all of your needs. It could be the perfect time to give part or all of your personal testimony. Then you'll be opening up about your own experience instead of preaching to him. By refusing to take the bait, you can sometimes avoid the argument the other person may be hoping for. By not allowing yourself to be put off by your friend's anger, you'll demonstrate God's steadfast, unswerving love.

Tolerating Intolerant Tolerance

Ah, tolerance, the battle cry of the New-Agers.

New Age religion pops up everywhere in the entertainment industry. It's not a clearly defined belief system. The theology is not written down anywhere, and there is no specific guidebook. It's a feel-good faith concocted of a little truth, lots of good energy, bad vibes, spirit guides, the light within you, and crystals.

It embraces a little of almost all other religions but borrows chiefly from Hinduism and Buddhism. New-Agers take the warm and fuzzy concepts from these Eastern religions, ignore the bad, and merge them with Western civilization. They're not good Hindus; they're not good Buddhists. They're just surfers on the spiritual shopping network.

Ironically, many have so glamorized India (the birthplace of both Hinduism and Buddhism) that they have a view of the country that isn't even realistic. It's chic for New Age Americans to take trips to India to find inner peace. Yet India is one of the most chaotic nations in the world, with the highest poverty level, the highest death rate per capita, and one of the highest levels of pollution globally. So where's all the peace?

It's difficult to refute New Age beliefs because they're so vague, sometimes because their proponents haven't thought them through. If they did, they would realize that their beliefs have most likely come from opposing belief systems. Let's say a person wants to believe in reincarnation and do his devotional reading from the Koran, the Islamic holy book. One system says everything is relative; the other demands a belief in absolute truth. Opposing belief systems can't be reconciled. It just can't work.

New-Agers believe they are finding their own truth. Each person believes something slightly different from the next. There is no "God's absolute truth," just many gray areas of "our interpretation." Many roads lead to God, they say. Any one of them is fine; none are required. Aren't we all part of the same spiritual family? You worship whatever floats your boat, and I'll do the same. A truly enlightened person appreciates everyone's point of view and respects any belief system because it's true to the one who believes it. Get into yourself, they say. Find your own truth.

We have found that there is a double standard among these politically correct champions of tolerance: They embrace all belief systems *except Christianity.* "You can believe anything you want," they say. "You can even include Jesus in your belief structure. Just don't come at me with traditional, conservative Christianity. It's narrow-minded, patriarchal, and judgmental. You need to learn to be more open-minded."

How intolerant can some tolerant people be?

We have also found that a person's belief in the relativity of truth ends the minute he feels wronged. He may believe that it's not wrong for him to sleep with other men's wives. If those husbands think it's wrong, that's their problem. But just listen to him when someone sleeps with *his* wife: "Now, that's just plain wrong!"

The key to approaching an intolerant "tolerant" person is to say that Jesus is the *only* way to God. When you do, your listener will immediately prove that his self-proclaimed tolerance is a sham. Jesus is the mighty pusher off of fences for all things, including tolerance. Don't pick a fight, but understand that total tolerance, like atheism, is an indefensible position.

When you witness to a New-Ager, rely on your trusty personal testimony. He respects personal experience—his whole belief system is based on it. Your three-minute testimony may not convince, but

175

his own beliefs prevent him from attempting to refute it. Tell your story; clarify any misunderstood terms attached to Christianity (such as born-again or fundamentalist); and tell him how awesome Jesus is. Don't argue. Pray, trust the Holy Spirit, and rave about your Lord until it becomes contagious!

Jim Says: A friend of ours was witnessing to a woman, Joy, who was into self-realization. Joy quickly became ready to accept Jesus into her life because she was so hungry for truth, but she still wasn't clear about the difference between her old beliefs and the gospel. She now believed that Jesus was God, but she liked the peaceful environment that the self-realization center offered.

The day she became a Christian, Joy was meditating in the garden of the self-realization fellowship. She decided she wanted Jesus to take over her life, so she prayed for salvation right there by the New Age temple, surrounded by other people who were meditating. Miraculously, after that prayer Joy never had the desire to go back to that place. That "peaceful" New Age environment suddenly left her empty.

Confounding the Cults

Many people are honestly seeking truth. They are searching for Christ, but they don't realize it. Sometimes before they find Him, they find something else. Though it's a counterfeit, it promises to fill the void that set them on their quest in the first place. Like Joy, these people often cling to what is familiar or safe.

Satan wins a great victory when he convinces people that a false religion is true by taking some of God's truths and twisting them a bit. In *The Cults, How to Respond*, Hubert F. Beck says, "Cult members are looking for meaning in life and a place where they belong. Unfortunately, they often end up both imprisoned and exploited by the cult."[5]

We are not here to list all of the cults or to talk about what they are and what they believe. But we do want you to become familiar with the various cults around the world. Learn how they differ from Christianity and be prepared to use what you learn. Then when you talk with a person who is involved in a cult, you can respond wisely. When you take a stand, do so "with gentleness and reverence," but also with clarity and confidence.

Hubert F. Beck gives us insight into cult followers:

> Rigidity of belief, an alternate and sometimes strange lifestyle, and an unwillingness to engage in conversation while pressing their understandings upon their hearers are what one frequently encounters when confronted by members of cults.[6]

Be aware that it can be quite difficult to talk to cult members without undue anger, stress, and resistance on their part. Usually they know only one way to tell what they believe, so they can't tolerate anything that breaks the flow. Don't get too involved in an emotional conversation.

And watch out for their cult training: Many cults arm their members with a dazzling line of arguments that can leave the Christian sputtering and confused. It's best to love them, refuse to argue, and pray for the Lord to soften their hearts and reveal His truth to them. Remember, these people came to their false beliefs out of a sincere hunger for true ones. God willing, they can still find their way home. We can't be arrogant, either. When someone from a cult is talking to us, we must be aware that we don't have the answers to all the tough questions. We just have to stand firm on the basic truths.

Jesus is the litmus test for distinguishing any cult from true Christianity. Cults have many wrong beliefs, but they all pale in comparison to the great error of misrepresenting Him. So if you really want to cut to the quick with a cult member, start talking about Jesus Christ. Ask who he says Jesus is and how he thinks a person can inherit eternal life. Ask him what he believes about the divinity of Christ.

As we have said several times, using the name of Jesus can trigger any number of reactions. Jesus' name is powerful and sharper than any two-edged sword (Hebrews 4:12). So when you bring it up, you could be setting off an explosion. On the other hand, if you avoid talking about Him, you'll never get anywhere and you've missed the key point in sharing your faith. Take out your sword, stand firm, and watch the Lord's deliverance.

By the way, here is a ready answer should cult members come knocking at your home. They're ready to launch into their scripted lines, fully expecting to blow away the poor soul who comes to the door. But you can take back the offensive—lovingly, of course. Start asking them about Jesus. Ask specifically who they say Jesus is and who they say He isn't. Then watch them twitch. As they start to make their retreat, you might even invite them in so you can talk to them about the real Jesus Christ.

On the surface many cults appear so similar to Christianity that even some Christians think they're okay. Adherents of Jehovah's Witnesses and Christian Science, for example, use a lot of the same words we hear in church every Sunday. They sound right. They read the Bible. So what's the problem?

Cults may use the same terms we do, but they give them different meanings. Jehovah's Witnesses, for example, will say they believe the same things about Jesus we do. They will even say Jesus is divine. But what they mean is that Jesus is *a* god, not the one true God. Take a look at John 1:1 in their special version of the Bible. It reads, "and the Word was a god." All other versions of the Bible read, "and the Word was God." Small change; huge difference.

The cult that fools most Christians today is the Church of Jesus Christ of Latter-Day Saints, or Mormonism. It has the appearance of a solid family-based faith. It attracts clean, smart, decent people who are even told they are Christians. (Never mind that they're also told they're gods.) Since the Mormons we know don't know what goes on in the inner sanctums of their Temple, they consider it an insult to be told that the *Book of Mormon* contradicts Christianity.[7]

It's a good idea for you to read up on cults. We've provided a starting point for you here. But in the end, it's what you know about the truth, not what you know about the lies, that will count.

CULT RESOURCES ON THE INTERNET

Christian Apologetics & Research Ministry	www.carm.org/dcults.htm
Christian Research Institute	www.equip.org
Watchman Fellowship Online	watchman.texan.com/watchman.htm

When the U.S. Treasury trains someone to identify counterfeit currency, the trainers don't spend time pointing out all of the various fake bills in circulation. All they do is to get the trainee so familiar with the real dollar that anything else stands out instantly as an obvious fake.

That's your job as a Christian. You have to get so familiar with the truth that any counterfeit is immediately obvious. If you want to delve a bit into the principal beliefs of any of the false religions, don't hesitate. But it's not necessary in order to lead a cult member to Jesus.

We encourage you to pray before, during, and after any conversation with someone who is involved in a cult. You want your words of truth to be heard clearly and precisely, and you need the Lord to give you those words.

Appealing to the Apathetic

We have found that hostile people are not the most difficult to reach; apathetic people are. The opposite of love isn't hate; it's apathy.

Apathetic people have hardened their hearts to the gospel so much that they no longer even react. They think that all people have the right to believe whatever they want. Anything is okay with them as long as others leave them alone. It's a type of numb indifference that has no foundation in any philosophical belief. Therefore, they push aside anything we say about Jesus with "that's what you believe; that's not what I believe."

Mark McCloskey, in his book *Tell It Often, Tell It Well,* describes this type of person as "the self-fulfillment secularist":

He is a child of a culture that has systematically laid a foundation for, and catered to, those who desired to interpret their lives from a purely materialistic perspective, which holds that any meaning, purpose or ultimate fulfillment is to be found in the worship and service of the finite.... He is seen as a one-dimensional consumer, a "need machine" that exists for the opportunity to have needs met.... Questions of eternal destiny and life's true meaning are bothersome sidetracks to his goal of "getting ahead".... We may find this person quite indifferent to spiritual issues because of his preoccupation with the needs of the here and now. Some may be very happy with their lives as they see a certain degree of success in meeting their goals. This spurs them on to an even greater commitment to their philosophy of life.[8]

We're sure you know some of these people. They're the ones who are singularly focused on their drive to succeed. They often have more material things than you have, and they live a flashier life because that's their priority and their god. They appear to have everything one could dream of, so there's no room or need for God. In fact, they believe that they either have everything or they're on their way to getting it. "Who has time to worry about God?"

What in the world do you say to these people? Here's something to remember about your apathetic friend: He is watching you, wondering why you handle tough circumstances differently than he does and how you could possibly be happy with less than he has. And he's quietly waiting for you to dump your silly faith and start living it up. He is secretly convinced that someday you'll see the light and outgrow this phase.

Therefore, the longer you stay consistent in your faith and continue to put God first, the more intrigued he will be. In the quiet of his room at night, he'll begin to compare his life with yours and notice differences that he would never admit to you or himself in the light of day. Your priorities will in some way appeal to him.

Even though he doesn't seem at all interested, you are witnessing by being his friend, serving him, and being open and honest about your faith. Don't hold back from expressing your beliefs about the Lord and how He works in your life. But don't preach, either. Just be yourself. The Holy Spirit is alive and well and working all the time, and God's Word does not return void (Isaiah 55:11).

The apathetic are the toughest non-Christians to reach with the gospel because they just don't see a need. They are far from fertile soil for the seed—but that doesn't mean they're hopeless. They

181

require long-term cultivating. Begin praying for God to show your apathetic friends their need for Him. Prayer is the key to unlocking the apathetic heart!

The Well-to-Do

The most intimidating person to talk to about Jesus is one who *appears* to have it all together because he has a lot of money and possessions. On the surface, he seems to have a much better life than you do. He is the world's picture of success, and he makes you feel that you don't have the right or the guts to tell him he needs God.

But appearances can be deceiving. Have you ever heard about someone who did something completely out of character, just totally flipped out, and later you heard that he'd been fooling everyone, living a double life? How many celebrities check themselves into rehab centers? Just because someone has the world's version of happiness doesn't mean he has anything close to the serenity you have.

Without Christ, even kings and princes walk in darkness. No one who is without Christ can ever be truly fulfilled. Henrietta Mears said, "The happiest people in the world are those who are in the center of God's will. The most miserable are those who are not doing God's will."[9] Believe that. Let it sink in. A person who symbolizes success to you—or to the world, anyway—is utterly, inescapably miserable if Jesus does not dwell in him. If he doesn't know that, it's because he has no point of reference.

Don't be intimidated by anyone. In God's eyes, no one is cooler, hipper, or more together than anyone else. We are all sinners. In His love, Jesus paid the ransom for everyone, great and small.

So how do you get through to these people? You can't change their lifestyle, their choices, or their stuff. All you can do is to tell them the truth that mankind needs God and that we were all created with a hole inside that only Jesus Christ can fill.

The deeper you dig with someone like this, the more you uncover. Keep at it. Stand firm. Keep praying. Learn his story. Cultivate a friendship. Encourage him to read Ecclesiastes, a book written by Solomon, a disillusioned man who "had everything." Sooner or later, it will become evident to your friend that you have something very special—something money can't buy.

Karen Says: Dawn was freaking out. As a member of our class, she was praying each week for a friend to come to Christ. One day she admitted that she believed the friend she was praying for had a better life than she did. This was making Dawn's prayer time extremely difficult and her motivation to reach out to her friend almost nonexistent.

She told the class about her friend: a wealthy, successful, beautiful, single businesswoman. Everything this woman touched turned to gold. This person even felt sorry for Dawn, a struggling actress who fought depression. Dawn didn't even want to tell her she was a Christian. Why in the world would she want what Dawn had?

We started asking Dawn questions about her successful friend. Did she want to get married? Did she have goals in her life that she had not yet reached? What were her struggles, obstacles, or systems for coping with problems in life?

Dawn began to see that she had to get to know her friend better. She needed to find out what really made her tick, what her spiritual background was, and what her expectations of life were. She would then be wiser about how to approach her with the Good News.

Knowing her friend would also allow Dawn to be open about her own life. She could explain how her faith in Jesus Christ is the only thing that gets her through tough days, hard decisions, and unmet expectations. Suddenly Dawn saw that when it came to some of the core issues of life, she might have something to offer her friend after all.

The Gen-Xer

This unique generation of people deserves its own section. As a group, they are not usually understood. Just as the hippies confounded the adults in the sixties, so this twenty-to-thirty-something generation now bewilders older adults.

Because they appear indifferent to traditional messages, some Christians consider Gen-Xers apathetic. But it may be that they just need to hear the message in a different way. In *The Power of Story,* Leighton Ford says that Generation X is "an impatient, pessimistic, amusement-centered generation...and the old evangelistic approaches won't work."[10]

By and large, Gen-Xers don't want to be lectured to; they won't be preached at; and they're bored with facts, figures, and statistics. So how can you talk to these people about Jesus? Do what Jesus did. Tell them stories. Ford says, "Narrative evangelism—the telling of the Story of God—is the key to reaching the hearts and minds of Generation X."[11]

This is your chance to tell your story and His story. Tell Gen-Xers your personal testimony. They'll love it, and they won't be bored, because no testimony is boring and they love stories.

Keep it short—like, maybe three minutes? Not everyone in this sound-bite generation has a long attention span. Transition from your story to His story, the plan of salvation. Stories, stories, stories. Maybe tell Paul's conversion story from Acts. Tell one of Jesus' parables. Tell four or five. Be creative and know that "narrative evangelism" is an exciting way to witness to anyone—especially a Gen-Xer.

Helping the Chosen to Choose

The entertainment business in Hollywood is run predominantly by Jewish people. They are proud to be Jewish, and we have received a variety of responses from them about Christianity and the person of Jesus.

Jewish people are very aware of their heritage and the suffering their people have experienced throughout history. They are often so committed to their people and culture that they can't hear the truth about Jesus. Or if they do, cultural pressure and family allegiance prevents them from accepting it.

It may surprise you that some of them don't even believe there is a God. The Jewish people we know regard themselves as cultural, not religious, Jews because their primary commitment is to one another and to the Jewish community at large instead of to a religion.

Dr. Arnold Fruchtenbaum says, "Israeli law is very clear on who is not a Jew. It is totally unclear on who is a Jew." He also quotes an atheist, Commander Benjamin Shalit of the Israeli Navy, who defines Jewishness on the following basis:

Religious observance is not part of the concept of Jewishness and the principal test of Jewishness is deliberate and declared association and identification with the Jewish people, its history, language, culture, and inheritance.... Anyone who declares himself to be a Jew by nationality is a Jew, even if he be an atheist, with the reservation however that he should not be so registered if he declares that he belongs to some other religious denomination. Jewishness...is not a biological question but one of historical, sentimental, and intellectual identification.[12]

Many Jews do not acknowledge the existence of God or adhere to any religious faith whatsoever. However, mentioning Jesus' name—even to Jews who do not embrace Judaism—creates division. His name is especially powerful to the Jew.

Regardless of what they believe, the Jews are still God's chosen people (Romans 11:26), so we need to understand their place in His plan. God still upholds His end of the covenant, looks to them as His own, and gives them great favor. If we could truly understand this and respect and love the Jews as the tree onto which God has graciously grafted us, we would treat these special people more respectfully in our relationships and conversations (see Romans 11:17–21).

Karen Says: My Jewish friend and producing partner was distantly supportive of my faith. She told me that her parents had sent her to parochial schools in order to give her the best education. However, some of the kids called her "Christ Killer" or "Jesus Killer" just because she was Jewish.

Suddenly I understood her hesitancy to embrace my faith. Her experience began my search into the complicated and delicate relationship between Christians and Jews. What I have learned since then is that there are more areas of mutual misunderstanding than I ever knew existed.

9

The three of us stand in awe of God's faithfulness to the Jews, even when they don't acknowledge that their blessings are from Him. We love to tell our Jewish friends and colleagues that we almost envy God's relationship with them. Jewish people who accept Jesus as their personal Savior (so-called completed Jews or Jewish believers) have the best of both worlds. They get to be members of God's original chosen people—and live with Jesus! What more could there be?

Love the Jewish people because of our common heritage. Let there be no bad feelings between us just because they are Jewish and we are Christian. Jesus was a Jew. He came to Israel, for Israel (Matthew 15:24), and He gave His life for them—His own people. We should thank the Jews for allowing us to come along for the ride, getting all that God gave them first, just because of His grace. When you look at it that way, it becomes exciting to talk to the Jewish people about their blessed and exciting heritage.

Rabbinic Debate

This may be the only time we will say it's okay to get into an argument about Jesus. Many Jewish people love an intellectual challenge. If you give them one, more often than not they will take it on. But you'd better be ready to slug it out, because if you back down about your beliefs, it will reflect on your commitment to Jesus and on how seriously they take you.

Jewish people don't respect wimps. They admire fighters, go-getters, people who don't take no for an answer even when they're holding an unpopular position. Jews have great intellectual pride. They respect intelligence, success, and initiative. Their lives reflect these priorities. When you can come alongside a Jewish friend or coworker and live out these qualities in your Christian walk, he will notice.

On the other hand, be aware of their preconceived notions about Jesus. Many Jewish people have been taught that Christians hate them, or that they created a religion to stop Judaism from spreading, or that Jesus was a political figure who failed. Only atheist Jews deny that Jesus existed. The typical cultural Jew believes that Jesus did live and was even a political leader, but that He lost power and died, leaving a mess and a divided nation behind.

What Do the Scriptures Say?

A powerful way to talk about Jesus with Jewish people is to discuss the sixty-six major prophecies in the Old and New Testaments that predict and explain His life and death. Remember, the Jewish faith embraces the Old Testament, but entirely dismisses the New Testament. The majority of Jewish people have never even opened the New Testament. So you'll have to make your case from the portion of the Bible they accept.

And just because they accept the Old Testament, don't assume they are familiar with all of it. Did you know that in almost every synagogue, the fifty-third chapter of Isaiah—the one chapter with more prophecies about Jesus than any other chapter in the Old Testament—is not read? When we asked a Jewish leader why this was so, he said that there's no reason to read it because through the centuries rabbis have never read it. According to him, the content isn't the issue. The issue is the tradition: Since Isaiah 53 has never been read before, there is no reason to start now.

The Old Testament was written hundreds of years before Jesus was born in Bethlehem. Portions of it were written thousands of years before. Yet all sections of it make predictions about the coming Messiah.

What are the odds that someone could correctly predict something about you a thousand years before you were born? What if someone made sixty or more predictions about you? What are the odds they would all be correct? One mathematician figured that the odds of someone fulfilling just eight of the sixty major prophecies concerning the Messiah would be one in 100,000,000,000,000,000.

How big is that number? The odds are the same as if you covered the entire state of Texas with silver dollars stacked a foot high, printed on one of the coins the phrase, "You've just won the Publisher's Clearinghouse Sweepstakes," and asked someone to ride a white horse haphazardly through the stack, lean over once at random, and pick up that one special coin. That's just for eight correct predictions. What would it be for sixty-six?

Can anyone still say that Jesus was just a good man who gave us some nice Hebrew proverbs?

Here are just eighteen of the sixty-six prophecies fulfilled by Jesus Christ:

1. *The Messiah would be born in Bethlehem.* Prophesied in Micah 5:2. Fulfilled in Matthew 2:1–6 and Luke 2:1–20.
2. *The Messiah would be born of a virgin.* Prophesied in Isaiah 7:14. Fulfilled in Matthew 1:18–25 and Luke 1:26–38.
3. *The Messiah would be a prophet like Moses.* Prophesied in Deuteronomy 18:15, 18–19. Fulfilled in John 7:40.
4. *The Messiah would enter Jerusalem in triumph.* Prophesied in Zechariah 9:9. Fulfilled in Matthew 21:1–9 and John 12:12–16.
5. *The Messiah would be rejected by His own people.* Prophesied in Isaiah 53:1–3 and Psalm 118:22. Fulfilled in Matthew 26:3, 4; John 12:37–43; and Acts 4:1–12.
6. *The Messiah would be betrayed by one of His followers.* Prophesied in Psalm 41:9. Fulfilled in Matthew 26:14–16, 47–50, and Luke 22:19–23.
7. *The Messiah would be tried and condemned.* Prophesied in Isaiah 53:8. Fulfilled in Luke 23:1–25 and Matthew 27:1, 2.
8. *The Messiah would be silent before His accusers.* Prophesied in Isaiah 53:7. Fulfilled in Matthew 27:12–14; Mark 15:3–4; and Luke 23:8–10.
9. *The Messiah would be struck and spat on by His enemies.* Prophesied in Isaiah 50:6. Fulfilled in Matthew 26:67, 27:30, and Mark 14:65.

10. *The Messiah would be mocked and insulted.* Prophesied in Psalm 22:7, 8. Fulfilled in Matthew 27:31–44 and Luke 23:11, 35.

11. *The Messiah would be put to death by crucifixion.* Prophesied in Psalm 22:14, 16, 17. Fulfilled in Matthew 27:31 and Mark 15:5, 20.

12. *The Messiah would suffer with criminals and pray for His enemies.* Prophesied in Isaiah 53:12. Fulfilled in Matthew 27:38; Mark 15:27–28; and Luke 23:32–34.

13. *The Messiah would be given vinegar and gall.* Prophesied in Psalm 69:21. Fulfilled in Matthew 27:34 and John 19:28–30.

14. *Others would cast lots for the Messiah's garments.* Prophesied in Psalm 22:18 and Psalm 34:20. Fulfilled in Matthew 27:35 and John 19:23–24.

15. *The Messiah's bones would not be broken.* Prophesied in Exodus 12:46. Fulfilled in John 19:31–36.

16. *The Messiah would die as a sacrifice for sin.* Prophesied in Isaiah 53:5–12. Fulfilled in John 1:29; 11:29–52; Acts 10:43 and 13:38–39.

17. *The Messiah would be raised from the dead.* Prophesied in Psalm 16:10. Fulfilled in Acts 2:22–32 and Matthew 28:1–10.

18. *The Messiah would ascend to God's right hand.* Prophesied in Psalm 110:1. Fulfilled in Mark 16:19 and Luke 24:50–51.

Reaching Those Closest to You

The Unsaved Church Member

As an important reminder, the first wrong assumption we can make about someone is that he is a Christian just because he says so. We aren't suggesting that you question a person's relationship with the Lord. But we also don't want you to assume from his casual comments that he has one. Just because you've been to the pool doesn't mean you can swim. If you grew up in a garage, that doesn't make you a car. Just because you were brought up in a Christian home or are an American who isn't Jewish doesn't mean you are a Christian!

Jim Says: Shelly took our ten-week witnessing class. She enjoyed it, but when it came to writing her three-minute testimony, she really struggled. She kept putting it off, saying that she couldn't quite get it right.

Over the course of the class, as Shelly listened to the other class members giving their testimonies, it slowly dawned on her that they had something she didn't have. She couldn't write the story of how she came to Christ because she'd never come to Christ! All the others had come to a point in their lives when God had changed them. Her life had never changed.

One night Shelly went home from class, leaned against her front door, and asked the Lord to change her. At that moment, God made her a new creature. Shelly quickly grew into a vital Christian whose life truly did change, and she is now a powerful ambassador for Christ in her life and work.

Thinking you're a Christian and really turning your life over to the Lord are two completely different things. Too often we miss divine appointments with needy friends or acquaintances because we assume they're already saved. These people need to know the difference; they need to know Jesus. A good question to ask at this point is: "Do you have a *personal* faith? It's very easy for people to attend church without ever having a personal relationship with Christ. What could be more tragic than a person spending a lifetime in church and an eternity in hell?

You might see a church friend falling apart in his personal life, but you don't want to lecture him about things you assume he already knows, so you never talk to him about Jesus. Don't assume that if someone says he's a Christian that his spiritual muscle is in top shape.

Get to really know your Christian friends, ask them questions, and find out their stories, just as you would pre-Christians. But also pray for them and pray with them. We're told to hold one another accountable. We need to be iron sharpening iron (Proverbs 27:17).

Are you a Christian? Have you given up your fight and asked Jesus to become your personal Lord and Savior? Have you ever considered what your relationship with Jesus really is? And, if so, have you surrendered the driver's seat to Him? Examine yourself to see if your faith is really genuine.

If you find yourself sweating right now, don't freak out. Just turn back to chapter 7, go through one of those explanations of the plan of salvation, and pray something like the sinner's prayer. Then call a friend and tell him the good news!

Jim Says: Karen and I invited Greg, a new friend, to a weekend seminar on how to share our Christian faith. When we broke up into pairs to discuss and write down our personal testimonies, I went with Greg.

I told him my testimony, then he began telling me his. He was struggling through it and got only as far as explaining his life without Christ when he broke out into a sweat and stopped talking. He finally looked up and said, "I don't think I'm a Christian. I can't go on with this until I become a Christian."

I asked him if he was ready right then. He said yes, and I got the privilege of leading him through the plan of salvation and praying with him. Greg held my hand tightly in his sweaty hands. When he finished praying, he opened his eyes, wiped away his tears, and finished telling me his testimony!

When you meet a stranger who says he is a Christian, don't always accept that as truth either. Ask those probing questions and listen carefully. You don't have to ask whether he'd go to heaven if he died tonight, but you can still fish around. Ask what Jesus is teaching him lately. Pray for wisdom to discern where he is spiritually. Especially, ask the Lord to use you in the life of any person whose life is full of frustration and empty of fruit.

You may find someone who is immature in the faith—someone you can move toward a surer walk with Christ. This is what Priscilla and Aquila did with Apollos in Acts 18:24–26. You don't want to miss an opportunity to tell someone how to gain that eternal relationship and how to live a richer and more vital life as a child of God. It would break our hearts if there were other people like Shelly and Greg in our lives, and we never offered them the Good News.

Sorry, Wrong Number

Has a Christian ever shared his faith with you? Have you ever had some really nervous yet caring person start to tell you about Jesus, not knowing that you were already a believer? If so, isn't it wonderful! It's much better to talk about Jesus to everyone—and even end up witnessing to a Christian—than to miss a divine appointment with someone because you assume he doesn't need to hear it.

Please understand that we do not want a holier-than-thou attitude of checking out people's faith. Don't go hunting for unbelievers who think they're Christians. Just be so excited about your faith that someone who is not a Christian will soon see the difference and want what you have.

Your Family

We have saved this for last because it's often the most challenging and most emotional of issues. Jesus Himself said, "No prophet is accepted in his own home town" (Luke 4:24).

The dynamics in a family can sometimes cause a stronger emotional response to the gospel than would occur in a conversation with others. Family members are deeply entwined in each other's lives, and the power of the gospel can touch a nerve that would never be touched if someone outside the family said the same thing.

We've said that the name of Jesus is like nuclear fission. Now we add to this the turmoil that bubbles just under the surface of many family relationships. When the two combine, there can be megareactions and fatal fallout.

You know the members of your family. Pray for wisdom and the right words to say at the right time. Pray for other Christians to come into their lives. Pray for their hearts to be prepared for a divine appointment, then always be ready to give an account for the hope that you have within you. But apply extra gentleness and great reverence.

We who have the Spirit understand these things,
but others can't understand us at all. How could they?
1 CORINTHIANS 2:15–16A

Victorya Says: We have a friend, Scott, who became a Christian as a teenager. He'd been raised in a non-Christian home, so when he got saved, the first thing he did was run to tell his family the great thing that had happened to him. He found his younger sister first and told her about Jesus. She wanted Jesus, too. Within hours of his own sinner's prayer, Scott got to lead his sister in it.

Then the two of them went to their parents, expecting the rest of the dominoes to fall. But their parents were not interested. They were happy for their children, but didn't want it for themselves. Scott couldn't understand why someone wouldn't want the gift he'd received.

Over the years, Scott and his sister prayed for their parents. When opportunities arose, they would witness to them. Sometimes they made opportunities. But nothing seemed to change.

Scott decided to change strategies. Instead of being in his parents' faces with the gospel, he would just live it out before them and pray for them. He would tell them what decisions he was facing and how the Bible was instructing him in which way to go. He would tell them about the things Jesus had taught him through hard situations. It was nonthreatening because he wasn't asking anything of them. Scott was able to talk about Jesus all day long with his parents without causing their defenses to go up.

After seventeen years, Scott's dad finally came to Christ. It was in another state and through another Christian, but Scott didn't care. His prayers had been answered!

Closing

There is nothing more thrilling than being used by God in the life of a family member who becomes a Christian. There is nothing sadder than having family arguments about Jesus.

Just live out your Christian faith before the members of your family. Show them God's love through random acts of kindness. Give them Bibles as gifts so that they can read about what you believe, if they so choose. Don't hide your faith, and don't water down the message when they ask you questions, but be wise in not offering information when it may not be wanted. And never stop praying for the ones you love the most.

They may not really be such tough nuts to crack.

1.   Ravi Zacharias, *Can Man Live Without God?* (Nashville, Tenn.: Word Publishing, 1994), 17.
2.   Ibid.
3.   C. S. Lewis, *Mere Christianity* (New York: Macmillan Publishing Co, 1943), 47.
4.   Lee Strobel, *What Would Jesus Say?* (Grand Rapids, Mich.: Zondervan Publishing House, 1994), 126.
5.   Hubert F. Beck, *The Cults: How to Respond* (St. Louis: Concordia Publishing House, 977), 24.
6.   Ibid., 32.
7.   An excellent book to give to someone who is a Mormon or investigating Mormonism is J. A. C. Redford, *Welcome All Wonders,* a sensitive, well written, thoroughly enjoyable book. Redford is a well-known composer and can be reached on the Internet at www.jacredford.com.
8.   Mark McCloskey, *Tell It Often, Tell It Well* (San Bernardino, Calif.: Here's Life Publishers, 105.
9.   Bill Bright, *Witnessing without Fear,* (San Bernardino, Calif.: Here's Life Publishers, 1987), 25.
10.   Leighton Ford, *The Power of Story* (Colorado Springs, Colo.: NavPress Publishing Group, 1994), 47.
11.   Ibid., 48.
12.   Dr. Arnold Fruchtenbaum, "Jewishness and Hebrew Christianity," *Jerusalem Post* (25 November 1968), reprinted as a pamphlet. Dr. Fruchtenbaum is the founder of a Bible institute in Israel and Ariel Ministries in San Antonio, Texas.

CHAPTER TEN

Tools for Your Tool Belt

I have hidden your word in my heart,
that I might not sin against you.
PSALM 119:11

Jim Says: On the first day of our witnessing class, Carl told us that he was excited about the class but that he couldn't memorize Scripture. I asked him to try anyway and said that we would encourage him.

Every week we passed around a red cup full of strips of paper with a different Bible reference written on each one. The students took turns drawing slips and quoting the verses from memory. Though extremely reluctant at first, Carl found that he could do it. He got better and better, more and more confident. In time he not only nailed the required verses, he even started memorizing bonus verses.

By the end of the ten-week class, Carl had memorized all the verses, and then some. By the end of the year, he had memorized one hundred Scriptures. For the following five years, he returned each year to put one hundred new references in a red cup and recite the verses back to us.

A few years ago, after many red cups full of memorized Scripture verses, Carl unexpectedly got cancer of the tongue. As he was being wheeled to surgery to have most of his tongue removed, he felt Jesus lovingly whisper, "You of little faith, why are you so afraid?" (Matthew 8:26, NIV). He felt immediate comfort and continued on in perfect peace. He later said that never could have happened if he hadn't memorized that verse.

Today, Carl is cancer free and has learned to talk again. He continues to put God's words in his heart because he has learned that those verses are his real strength.

Megamemory

Does the thought of memorizing Scriptures bring back nightmares of pop quizzes in school? Does it make you break out in a cold sweat?

In this chapter, we're going to give you three tools you'll find very useful when you step up to talk about Jesus. Memorizing Scripture is one of them. Don't let Carl intimidate you—a willing volunteer is all God wants. Convincing someone of his need for Christ is God's job. But when you're out there talking about Jesus, wouldn't you feel more secure standing atop a great heap of familiar Scriptures instead of balancing on a tottering pile of vague references?

Americans are spoiled. We take our freedoms for granted, especially our freedom to read the Bible in any version anytime we feel like it. There are many places in this world where that freedom does not exist, and there is no guarantee it will always exist here. If you hide the Word of God in your heart now, no matter what the future brings, you will be prepared. The more Scripture you have in your head, the more you can bring to mind when talking to others.

Someone who really knows his stuff impresses all of us. It makes us pay attention to his position, even if we are predisposed to dismiss it. So it is with memorized Scripture in a discussion of spiritual matters. The verses you've committed to memory are like your CD collection. The Holy Spirit can select the exact one He'd like you to use at that moment. The larger your collection, the better He can suit the Word of God to the situation.

If you don't make a commitment to study the Bible and learn Scripture, how are you going to be equipped to present a defense for the hope that is in you?

Still, memorizing has to be more than a commitment. It has to be a desire. We can always find time in our lives to do the things we want to do. Want to memorize Scripture? Try it with a friend. Our friend Karen Leonard and her memory partner, who lives in a different state, phone each other weekly to recite that week's verses. They've been doing this for more than ten years, and they're getting closer to their goal of memorizing the entire New Testament.

Victorya Says: One of the easiest ways for me to memorize is with flash cards. It's also a great excuse to practice verses around my pre-Christian friends. One of my unbelieving business associates actually used to quiz me while we traveled across town to meetings. She would even tell me to slow down if I was quoting the verse too quickly. She made sure I knew that she did not share my faith; she was just trying to help me study.

For Christmas I gave her a Bible, hoping she would read it. For my birthday five months later I was astonished to receive a special homemade plaque of framed Scriptures on friendship. She told me that she had never read the Bible before she began to make the plaque, but she had opened it to pick out these verses for me.

I was so blessed and encouraged. I continue to pray for her to this day.

10

During the ten weeks of our class, each student writes out eighteen verses to memorize for the Bridge. They write them out on three-by-five-index cards, with the verse on one side and the reference on the other. Then they use them as flash cards for practice. You can also practice while you jog, drive, dress, put on makeup, cook, mow the grass—whenever. You can memorize Scripture anytime you have free "thinking time."

We challenge you to take at least five minutes a day out of your hectic schedule to memorize a verse. Just take one at a time and ask someone to quiz you. You can start with Philemon 6. Then go on to the verses from the Bridge. You'll find that after you memorize a verse, you'll start using it. And you might discover you have a gift you didn't know you had.

Armed with pocketfuls of Scriptures, you'll not only be able to give the person you're talking to something about Jesus right from God's Word, you'll also begin to gain confidence in doing the most important work there is.

Give away Those Bibles

The second tool for your witnessing tool belt is to give away Bibles. As you witness to someone, ask him if he owns a Bible. If he tells you that he doesn't but would consider reading it, rush out that very day and get him one, print his name on it, and deliver it to him as soon as you can. You will be sowing eternal seeds.

Victorya Says: Before I started teaching Karen and Jim's class, I was one of the class members. I remember that they encouraged each of us to begin giving Bibles as gifts to our unbelieving friends. They also told us to make sure, when possible, to have the person's name printed on the cover of the Bible (most

Christian bookstores will do this for about five dollars).

At first I was intimidated. I thought that would be taking it too far. It was one thing to tell others what I believed, but I feared they would interpret the gift of a Bible as my trying to shove my beliefs down their throats. After Karen and Jim told several stories about their positive experiences of giving Bibles as gifts, I summoned up the courage and tried it out on a friend I had been telling about Jesus.

The gift was a hit! And the reaction to her name on the cover was even more incredible. She told me that I had no idea how much that meant to her. That was just the encouragement I needed. I haven't stopped since. I do it so often that one girlfriend nicknamed me the "Gideon of Hollywood." Out of the dozens of Bibles I've given away, I have not had one negative reaction!

Once you give someone a Bible, always offer directions. Never just give it with the nonverbal message, "Okay, I've done my part; you're on your own." There are few things scarier to an unbeliever or a new believer than a Bible. It's so thick! On the logical assumption that he's supposed to read it from start to finish, he'll probably open it to Genesis. But by the time he gets to Exodus, he's out of there! That would defeat the purpose for which you gave him the Bible.

Consider writing a personal note to let the recipient know that you want him to come to love this Book as much as you do. In the note encourage him to start with the book of John, which has the clearest and most concise explanation of how to become a Christian. We suggest that Jewish people begin in Matthew because it was written to Jews.

Recommend that he read the other Gospels after finishing the first one. Consider explaining that the four Gospels—Matthew,

Mark, Luke, and John—are biographies of Jesus. We believe it's important, first and foremost, that the person know who Jesus is. In addition to a personal note, we often include the handout "How Not to Be Overwhelmed Reading the Bible" (see end of chapter). This is a guide to reading the Bible that will be helpful to new readers. It's also good to put a Post-It note in the Gospel of John with the words "Start here!" on it.

So Many Translations!

When you walk into a Christian bookstore to buy your friend a Bible, the number of options to choose from may surprise you. There's the King James and the New King James, the *American Standard* and the *New American Standard, Today's English Version*, the New Century Version, *The Amplified Bible, The New Jerusalem Bible*, and *The Message*—just to name a few! How do you choose?

We recommend that you not give the original King James Bible. It was translated back in 1611! Full of *thees* and *thous*, its language is often too difficult for modern readers, especially seekers. You want something that is very clear but neither too scholarly nor too elementary. Something user-friendly.

We recommend either the New International Version (NIV) or the New Living Translation (NLT). The NLT is what we've used in this book. It's nonthreatening and easy to understand. The NIV is also excellent. If you're giving this Bible to an intellectual, the NIV—or even the *New American Standard Bible* (NASB)—would be just right.

The Gift for All Reasons

There are so many socially acceptable opportunities to give Bibles: weddings, births, birthdays, holidays, graduations, and other significant passages of life. Children's Bibles with big pictures and easy-to-read stories are great for baby gifts. The whole family will be reading them sooner than you know. However, you don't have to wait for times like these. We love to give people Bibles when they're going through tough times—especially after failed relationships or during illnesses. This is one of the most exciting gifts you can give. So get creative.

We know that some people to whom we've given Bibles have not yet read them, but we keep praying for them. We're amazed at some of the things they say out of the blue, such as, "You know, I still have that Bible you gave me. I know right where it is, and I'll get to it someday." Or "I haven't read it yet, but it sits right by my bed." Comments like these tell us that as we continue to pray, the Lord will nudge them to open it, and at just the right time they'll have it to turn to instead of something else that wouldn't lead them to the truth.

Victorya Says: A producer friend said he would read the Bible if only he had the time. But his days were filled with reading dozens of film scripts, and what he couldn't get done at the office he took home with him at night. The rest of his "free" time was spent in Los Angeles traffic. When I asked if he would consider listening to the Bible on audiocassettes, he laughed and said, "Okay, if they actually have it on cassettes, for you I'll listen." I had them delivered to his office the next day. The last time I spoke to him about it, he said he keeps them in the car and occasionally pops one in and listens.

10

The third tool we want to give you for your tool belt is a way to challenge pre-Christians to read the Bible for themselves.

Change Your Life in Thirty Days: The 30-Day Experiment

We've discovered that many people who say that they have read the Bible and rejected it haven't actually read it or have read only small portions without exploring them fully or with an open mind.

As an excuse to avoid studying the Bible, some people claim that they read it as a child and found it full of stories, wives' tales, dated references, contradictions, and legends. Their insistence that the Bible isn't valid often stems from a barely remembered, random reading, or, more likely, hearsay from others who also claim to have read it.

The Bible is a spiritual book. To the unsaved, it can seem tightly closed, like a lockbox. The spiritually undiscerning can never unearth its riches. Having said that, the Bible is still the most wonderful book for an unsaved person to read. It is actually alive—the very Word of God—and can cut through doubt and disbelief like a scalpel in the hands of a master surgeon. Like the name of Jesus, the Word of God contains explosive power—the power of creation and resurrection.

Therefore we encourage you to challenge your skeptical friend to read the Bible as a mature adult and not cling to his childhood beliefs about it. Remind him that we all believed things as children that as adults we know are not true. If he says he's already read the Bible, ask him to read it afresh. If he has never read it, ask him to begin to read it today.

Tell your friend that you respect his intelligence and that you are impressed that he's willing to search out a matter rather than blindly accept everything he hears. Suggest he start by reading only a portion of the Bible and lay out a simple reading plan for him.

We call this approach the 30-Day Experiment. It's a revision of

Dick Purnell's "31-Day Experiment," which we've organized into two different but equally effective approaches.[1] Version A is for the openly hungry seeker; version B is for the more apprehensive seeker. We have written a script for each version to give you an idea of how to challenge a pre-Christian to try this life-changing experiment.

The 30-Day Experiment (Version A)

"I ask you to read, with an open mind, a portion of the Bible for an hour every day for the next thirty days. Each day, before you begin to read, ask God this question: 'If You are for real—the only God—and Jesus really came down to earth for me personally, then I ask You to reveal Yourself to me and show me how to know You.' Then begin reading.

"Start with the book of John, the fourth book in the New Testament. After you finish John, go back to Matthew, then Mark, then Luke. These are four accounts of the life of Jesus. When you've completed these four books, continue on through the New Testament. I'll call you midmonth to see how you're doing.

"If your month isn't up when you get to the end, go back to the beginning and read the Old Testament straight through. If you do this every day, with an honest search for truth, I know you will be excited about what you find and what God will reveal to you."

The 30-Day Experiment (Version B)

"For the next thirty days, I ask you to read just one chapter a day of the Gospel of John. John is the fourth book of the New Testament. It has the best description of who Jesus is and why God sent Him down to earth. The book is only twenty-one chapters long, so if you read one chapter a day, you can skip weekends. Each day before you read the chapter, start with a simple request to God asking Him to please reveal Himself to you as you read.

"Continue this through the end of John, and by the end of the month I believe you'll have a new perspective of God, Jesus, and the Bible. I'll call you midmonth to see how you're doing. Go ahead and jot down any questions or struggles you have with it while you're reading. I'd love to talk with you about them either as you go or when you're done. But give it a shot and go into this commitment with the expectation that you might actually see God in a different light."

We have seen exciting results from both versions of this challenge. What's important is not the length of time your friend spends reading each day, but his willingness to bring God into the experience, even if he isn't sure he believes in Him. If after thirty days your friend finds out nothing more about God, he can go on his way knowing he's given Him a fair try. But believe us, if your friend stays committed to the challenge, that won't happen.

This challenge will help you discern who is really seeking God and who is giving Him lip service. You'll have friends and associates who say they'll take the challenge but then read a couple of days and quit, or never even begin. Those people just aren't ready yet.

If a person won't take you up on the challenge, tell him that if he ever finds that he's ready or curious to find out who God is, he should remember this experiment and try it. If he decides not to try it, don't act annoyed or discouraged. Remember, it's only your job to raise the flag. It's between God and that person whether or not he'll salute.

If someone you know does accept the challenge, be sure to follow up. Check on his progress midmonth and get together at the end to discuss his experience. Your personal involvement could be the most important element of all.

Some witnessing lends itself to the use of different tools. As a bonus, here are a few specialized tools for those special situations.

Bonus Tools

- The next time a solicitor comes to your door, buy something from him and then tell him how Jesus transformed your life. Maybe he'll leave with the greatest treasure of all.

- You're at a restaurant and the harried waitress comes to your table. Ask her name and then tell her that before you eat you're going to pray and that you'll pray for her too. Then be sure to do it. And of course, give her a big tip!

- Put *Happy Birthday, Jesus* on your Christmas cards.

- For kids' presents, give some of the latest and greatest videos available such as *Veggie Tales* or *McGee and Me.* There are many more that are also perfect for pre-Christian kids.

Cool Down

There now, was that so terrible? Memorization, giving away Bibles, and the 30-Day Experiment—three great tools for your belt. Now it's up to you to put them into action. Get some index cards, buy some Bibles, and try the 30-Day Experiment yourself to see how it works. Every step you take will get you closer to the Lord. The closer your relationship is with God, the more natural all these suggestions will become.

The following two-page spread, "How Not to Be Overwhelmed Reading the Bible," is a tool we developed to give to readers. Feel free to copy it and put it inside every Bible you give away.

How Not to Be Overwhelmed Reading the Bible

- **First and Always:** Ask God for understanding and insight. (Some call this *prayer.*) It was His idea to write the Bible in the first place, so we might as well ask Him to help us to understand it!
- **What to Know:** The Bible is a collection of sixty-six books written by numerous people who have had firsthand encounters with the living, personal God. It is split into two parts: the Old Testament and the New Testament. The Old Testament includes the account of Creation, the history of Israel, and many prophecies of the coming Messiah. The New Testament gives God's plan for man and the fulfillment of every Messianic prophecy in the person of Jesus Christ.
- **Where to begin:** The best place to begin reading is in the Gospels—the first four books of the New Testament. Matthew, Mark, Luke, and John give firsthand accounts of the life of Jesus. We recommend that a new reader begin with the Gospel of John, the clearest overview of the Bible. Then go back to Matthew and read the entire *New* Testament, followed by the *Old* Testament.

Reading for Bible History

- *GENESIS:* If you're a person who must start at the beginning, Genesis tells how God showed Himself in the creation of the world and the birth of the nation Israel. In Genesis 3:15, God foreshadows the future revelation of Himself in' His son, the Messiah. Its fulfillment is best described in the book of John.
- *GOSPEL OF JOHN:* This is a great summary of the life of Jesus. It's only about twenty-five pages long. The entire Gospel is best summed up in chapter three.
- *EXODUS:* Moses leads the people out of Egypt to Mount Sinai where God gives him the Ten Commandments. In the book of Exodus, the celebration of the Passover foreshadows Jesus.
- *ACTS:* Keeping in mind the Israelites' struggle to return to the Promised Land, read how the faith of this same people was established with the coming of Jesus as their Messiah.

Reading the Bible for Theology

- **ROMANS:** Paul answers the "big" questions of Christian life, including the issues of hope, strength, sin, perseverance, and grace.
- **PHILIPPIANS:** A letter written to new Christians on how to lead a life that is pleasing to God.
- **EPHESIANS:** Another terrific instruction letter on Christian conduct.
- **HEBREWS:** See how throughout the history of the nation of Israel God has always rewarded those who persevere in their life and in their belief in Him.
- **REVELATION:** Read only chapters 1 and 22 if you are a new Christian. In these two chapters Jesus talks about His return. The rest of Revelation is pretty much heavy-duty prophecy told in allegories and images.

Reading for Wisdom and Help

- **A PROVERB A DAY KEEPS THE FOOL AWAY:** One of the best success manuals ever in print is in the Old Testament. Proverbs—the book of wisdom—has thirty-one chapters. In addition to your daily devotions, it's a wonderful idea to read the chapter that corresponds to the day of the month in which you are reading.
- **PSALMS—THE PRAYER BOOK OF ANCIENT CHRISTIANS:** The Psalms have been used as a prayer and songbook for Christians since the days of its author, King David. If you want to learn how to pray, Psalms is a great place to go.

There is Something for Everyone

Here is where to find some of the best biographies:

- Adam and Eve (Genesis 1–6)
- Noah (Genesis 6–9)
- Abraham (Genesis 11–25)
- Jacob (Genesis 25–29)
- Joseph (Genesis 37–50)
- Moses (Exodus–Deuteronomy)
- Ruth (the book of Ruth)
- David (1 Samuel 16; 1 Kings 2:10; Psalms)
- Solomon (1 Kings 1–11, Proverbs)
- Esther (the book of Esther)
- Job (the book of Job)
- And most importantly: Jesus (Matthew–John)

1. Dick Purnell, *Growing Closer to God: A 31-Day Experiment* (Nashville, Tenn.: Thomas Nelson Publishers, 1993). Used by permission. Purnell is director of Single Life Resources, a ministry of Campus Crusade for Christ, which can be found on the Web at www.slr.org.

CHAPTER ELEVEN

Apologetics 101
A Crash Course in Truth

*The more one separates oneself from the canons
of the Christian church,
the further one distances oneself from the truth.*
IGOR STRAVINSKY

Jim's Nightmare

There you are in your high school biology class, trying to stay awake. Midway through the period, Mr. Greenbaum starts his sermon about the wonders of scientific advances and quantum mechanics.

Greenbaum knows his audience. He knows you are the treasurer of a Christian club on campus. So he stops at your desk and peers at you with his beady eyes from beneath his one continuous eyebrow. Then, in a moment of high drama, he clutches his pocket protector, stares at the ceiling, and exclaims, "How all of those simpleminded fundamentalists can cling to their pathetic little Bible stories in the face of scientific facts, I will never understand!"

His words echo in your mind the rest of the day. Is what you believe really true? Is it based on anything but Sunday school stories?

Have you bought into all of this Christianity stuff on blind, feeble faith? Is there no verifiable, scientific evidence for what you believe? Yes, there is!

But What If I'm Not Sorry?

There's good, hard data to substantiate the claims of the Bible. In this chapter, we'll give you dozens of reasons why what you believe is worthy of the faith of intellectual humans—like you.

Have you ever heard someone use the term *apologetics?* What does that mean? Does it mean you're supposed to apologize for Jesus? Of course not! Apologetics means a well-reasoned, formal defense of the gospel. Anytime you open your mouth in defense of the Bible or Christ, you are an apologist.

The little nuggets of truth in this chapter will give you evidence to support the hope that is in you. They represent only the tip of the iceberg of the historical, archaeological, logical, and scientific support for Christianity.[1] Hopefully, they will help you know why it is completely reasonable to believe the claims of the Bible. If you've been stuck in second gear ever since your close encounters in biology class, these truths will give you an assurance of what you believe.

But before we get to these truths, let's talk about the nonbelievers who ask those hard questions that stump us. Are they really reaching out to God?

Smoke Screens

"Could God create a rock so big He couldn't lift it?" "Can you prove that Mary really was a virgin when she had Jesus?" "How can the Bible be true when it has been mistranslated over and over again as it's been passed down from generation to generation?" "What proof is there that God loves me personally?"

Are these sincere questions, asked by someone who really wants the answers? Or are they just mind twisters designed to make the skeptic look clever, the Christian look foolish, and the issue go away?

Smoke screens are questions people ask when they really don't want to hear the answers. They want to avoid the truth so much that they divert their minds and yours by asking a list of questions intended to keep the conversation spinning. They use questions like a pole to stave off the real issues.

When you start hearing questions like these, be careful. Pray for discernment. You could be talking to a serious seeker of truth or to a person with a hard heart, oversized ego, and clever repartee. The same question can be a smoke screen in one instance and a legitimate question in another. The difference is in the heart of the questioner.

Watch your step. First, give people the benefit of the doubt and do your best to answer a couple of tough questions. If you discover that someone is posing them for entertainment or out of love for heated debate, give it up. You are probably not going to move that person even half a step closer to Jesus. Don't frustrate yourself trying to discuss your beliefs logically.

Ask the Lord for wisdom to be able to discern who is truly seeking and who is not. You must take a seeker's questions seriously. Either answer the best you can or get back to him with an answer from Scripture or from another person of faith. There are many obstacles with which people honestly struggle. And we should be there, walking alongside, offering any insight we might have. But you can't always tell—a skeptic might be using them as smoke screens. Discernment, discernment, discernment. Ask for wisdom and God will provide it (James 1:5).[2]

Help, I'm Stumped!

If a question has you stumped, the best you can do is to be honest. Be compassionate, patient, and encouraging. Reassure him that these are good and important questions and that you are willing to help him try to find answers.

Also, don't be afraid to say that you don't know if there *are* answers for some questions. In these instances, be honest with the seeker and admit your ignorance. We won't know some things until we get to heaven. Can you state with confidence that your dog Fluffy will be in heaven with you? Or tougher yet, can you explain why God allowed a sweet fifteen-year-old to be brutally raped?

Sometimes you have to let the seeker wrestle with some tough questions. Sometimes you'll be the one doing the wrestling. Just hang on to Jesus. Try to answer the person from Scripture and experience, but remind yourself that this isn't up to you. Pray that the Lord will reveal Himself to that person when he is ready to accept the truth.

Don't become impatient with a seeker. No one comes to the truth until God has opened his eyes. Be content to help him move one step closer to God, and accept that the timing is in God's hands.

Unsolved Mysteries

There are as many hard questions about life as there are people. Some gifted theologians have attempted answers to a few of the toughest ones. Here, we'll give you four from author Chuck Swindoll.[3]

Tough Question #1: What about the death of babies?

This question is extremely important to those who have lost an infant at birth or a little child who never reached an age of spiritual comprehension.

It's my understanding that small children who die before they are able to understand the basic issues of salvation and faith in the Lord Jesus go immediately into the presence of the Lord. No passage of Scripture is any clearer on this subject than 2 Samuel 12:23, where David says of his infant who has just died, "I shall go to him, but he will not return to me." The baby can't return to earth, but when David dies and enters the presence of the Lord, he will see his child.

Somehow, in God's wonderful plan, He has reserved in heaven a place for the precious infants and little people whose lives ended prematurely on this earth.

Tough Question #2: What about those who have never heard the gospel?

We must always be careful about stepping into the role of God. People you and I may think are in the family may not be—and vice versa. God alone knows the heart. He alone makes the final determination. Not all who call Him Lord will enter the kingdom. Conversely, not all who think they are lost actually are. Some who genuinely know Christ mistakenly assume that they've lost their salvation.

To answer this question, we need to remind ourselves of the basis of salvation. "If you confess with your mouth Jesus is Lord, and believe in your heart that God raised Him from the dead, you shall be saved; for with the heart man believes, resulting in righteousness, and with the mouth he confesses, resulting in salvation" (Romans 10:9–10). The only way to have eternal life with God is through faith in the Lord Jesus Christ. The marvel of God's plan is that He has an endless number of ways of reaching the lost. As they are reached and the Holy Spirit uses the truth of Scripture to convince them, they will believe.

Tough Question #3: *What about deathbed repentance?*

No one on earth can determine with absolute certainty the eternal destiny of another individual, so who is to say that no one can become a Christian at the end of his life?

Remember one of the thieves on the cross? He had lived the life of a criminal. But when he was confronted with the truth of Christ in his final hours, he accepted it, and Christ acknowledged his faith.

> One of the criminals hanging beside him scoffed, "So you're the Messiah, are you? Prove it by saving yourself—and us, too, while you're at it!"
>
> But the other criminal protested, "Don't you fear God even when you are dying? We deserve to die for our evil deeds, but this man hasn't done anything wrong." Then he said, "Jesus, remember me when you come into your Kingdom."
>
> And Jesus replied, "I assure you, today you will be with me in paradise." (Luke 23:39–43)

Tough Question #4: *How can a loving God send people to hell?*

This question implies that God treats mankind unfairly. If the question is posed as a foregone conclusion, that assumption needs to be dealt with first. Suffice it to say, it is not what Scripture teaches.

But if it's an honest question, and a person is struggling to reconcile God's loving character and hell's awful consequences, then I would begin by saying that God has established the ground rules. That's His sovereign right. As the creator of life, it is His divine right to decide that those who believe in Him will have eternal life with Him and that those who do not believe in His Son will not have eternal life with Him. Those who believe the message will inherit the blessedness of heaven. Those who reject the message will reap the consequences of their decision.

216

And lest you think God is callused and unconcerned about that possibility, you need to remember this: "The Lord is not slow about His promise, as some count slowness, but is patient toward you, not wishing for any to perish but for all to come to repentance" (2 Peter 3:9). If a person seems to think that God cruelly and gleefully dances about heaven as people are dumped into hell against their will, remind them of Peter's words. With patience and grace God offers the gift of eternal life and heaven to all who will accept it.

The Reliable Bible

The Bible is God's holy, infallible Word, and you can rest assured that modern translations of it are accurate and dependable. The following truths help build the case for the trustworthiness of the Bible.

TRUTH:

The Bible is the most accurate ancient document of all time, even though skeptics like to claim that its meaning has been altered over the millennia. They say that copying errors, negligence, and downright censorship have conspired to make the Bible completely unreliable.

We'll tell you why that's not possible. The Bible has been held sacred since Moses began to write it down. Through hundreds of years, faithful copyists have taken their task with grave earnestness, and elaborate restrictions have been placed on them to ensure absolute accuracy. Consider these few examples of the lengthy regulations for the Jewish Talmudist:

- A synagogue roll must be written on the skins of clean animals, prepared for the particular use of the synagogue by a Jew.
- These must be fastened together with strings taken from clean animals.

- Every skin must contain a certain number of columns, equal throughout the entire codex.
- The length of each column must not extend over less than forty-eight or more than sixty lines, and the breadth must consist of thirty letters.
- The whole copy must be first-lined; and if three words be written without a line, it is worthless.
- The ink should be black, neither red, green, nor any other color, and be prepared according to a definite recipe.
- An authentic copy must be exemplar, from which the transcriber ought not in the least deviate.
- No word or letter, not even a *yod*, must be written from memory, the scribe not having looked at the codex before him.
- Between every consonant the space of a hair or thread must intervene; between every new paragraph, or section, the breadth of nine consonants; between every book, three lines.
- The fifth book of Moses must terminate exactly with a line; but the rest need not do so.
- Besides this, the copyist must sit in full Jewish dress, wash his whole body, not begin to write the name of God with a pen newly dipped in ink, and should a King address him while writing that name he must take no notice of him.

TRUTH:

Moses spoke with divine knowledge that he couldn't have learned on his own. Thousands of years before the advent of modern science, he gave the events of Creation in perfect scientific order. Do you know what the probability is of a man who lived 8,000 years ago getting all eleven Creation events in the right order? One in 40 million!

TRUTH:

Earlier in this century antagonists of the Bible frequently came up with what they claimed were archaeological contradictions that made the Bible an unreliable document. Each new archaeological discovery, however, chips away at their list.

For example, some said there was no record of a census taken by Caesar Augustus at the time of Jesus' birth, as is recorded in Luke's Gospel. Just recently, archaeologists found a papyrus in Egypt that gave instructions for a Roman census at the time of Jesus' birth.

TRUTH:

Do you know why the 1947 discovery of the Dead Sea Scrolls (dated 125 B.C.) had such a tremendous impact? One reason was that the exactness of the Isaiah scroll provided solid proof that the Old Testament has not changed over time. A really loooooong time—like 1,000 years or so.

TRUTH:

The listing of the order of the kings who reigned during the Old Testament period is historically perfect. The odds of getting the order right by chance is one in 750,000,000,000,000,000,000,000,000.

TRUTH:

Did you know that all of the proper names in the Bible correspond exactly with every archaeological finding we have for the period between 2,000 and 4,000 years ago?

TRUTH:

In libraries around the world, there are many early, complete manuscripts of the Old Testament dating from more than a thousand years ago. The Cairo text (A.D. 916) is in the British

Museum and the *Babylonicus Petropalitanus* text (A.D. 1008) is in Leningrad, to mention just two. (Too bad they're in the reference section. They never let you check out any of the good books.)

TRUTH:

The John Ryland manuscript (A.D. 130) contains most of the book of John. This ancient parchment is located in John Ryland Library in Manchester, England. When you ask someone to read the Gospel of John, or quote a verse from it (i.e., John 3:16), it may help him to know that the Bible you just handed him or quoted from is historically accurate. The texts we read today are exactly the same, almost to the word, as the A.D. 130 texts. This sets the Bible apart from works that are confirmed oral traditions, such as Homer's *The Odyssey* and *The Iliad*.

TRUTH:

Other ancient writings and inscriptions corroborate the Bible. Many ancient authors wrote about Jesus. Flavius Josephus (born A.D. 37) was a Jewish historian and a Pharisee. In one of his writings he said:

Now there was about this time Jesus, a wise man, if it be lawful to call him a man, for he was a doer of wonderful works, a teacher of such men who receive the truth with pleasure. He drew over to him both many of the Jews, and many of the Gentiles. He was the Christ. When Pilate, at the suggestion of the principle men among us, condemned him to the cross, those who loved him at the first did not forsake him; for Jesus appeared to them alive again the third day; as the divine prophets had foretold these and ten thousand other wonderful things concerning him. And the tribe of Christians so named from him are not extinct at this day.[4]

📖 *TRUTH:*

The New Testament is written from primary sources. Eyewitnesses either wrote down what they had seen, or told someone who wrote down their accounts. Luke, for example, said that he wrote down the things he himself had carefully investigated (Luke 1:1). Such firsthand accounts refute arguments that the Bible consists of hand-me-down stories corrupted by oral tradition.

📖 *TRUTH:*

Did you know that though the Bible is much older than the works of Shakespeare, its accuracy has stood the test of time, while that of Shakespeare's works hasn't?

> It seems strange that the text of Shakespeare, which has been in existence [at least] two hundred and eight years, should be far more uncertain and corrupt than that of the New Testament, now over eighteen centuries old, during nearly fifteen of which it existed only in manuscript.... With perhaps a dozen or twenty exceptions, the text of every verse in the New Testament may be said to be so far settled by general consent of scholars, that any dispute as to its readings must relate rather to the interpretation of the words than to any doubts respecting the words themselves.[5]

Josh McDowell states that in Shakespeare's thirty-seven plays there are probably a hundred disputed readings, the interpretation of which materially affects the meaning of the passages in which they occur.[6]

No Apologies

We have put together a collection of powerful arguments to substantiate our belief in Christ. These are some of the most compelling reasons to believe we've yet found.

A word of warning: Use them as a means to steer conversations back to Jesus. What good is it to win every argument but never "win" a single soul? And please never let this information cause division between you and another Christian. We provide it to equip you to defend your position, but remember that love and prayer are more powerful than even the most articulate apologetic.

Liar, Lunatic, or Lord

Jesus cannot be considered just a good moral teacher. C. S. Lewis, who was a professor at Cambridge University and once an agnostic, wrote:

> I am trying here to prevent anyone saying the really foolish thing that people often say about him: "I'm ready to accept Jesus as a great moral teacher, but I don't accept his claim to be God." That is one thing we must not say. A man who was merely a man and said the sort of things Jesus said would not be a great moral teacher. He would either be a lunatic—on a level with the man who says he is a poached egg—or else he would be the Devil of Hell. You must make your choice. Either this man was, and is, the Son of God, or else a madman or something worse.[7]

Either, Or

Did you know that if Christ has not been raised from the dead our faith is useless (1 Corinthians 15:14)? Josh McDowell said:

> After more than 700 hours of studying this subject, and thoroughly investigating its foundation, I have come to the

222

Jesus Claims to be God

(TWO ALTERNATIVES)

CLAIMS WERE

FALSE

(TWO ALTERNATIVES)

He KNEW His claims were FALSE

He made a DELIBERATE MISREPRESENTATION

He was a LIAR

He was a HYPOCRITE

He was a DEMON

He was a FOOL, for He died for it

He DID NOT KNOW His claims were FALSE

He was SINCERELY DELUDED

He was a LUNATIC

CLAIMS WERE

TRUE

HE IS LORD

(TWO ALTERNATIVES)

You can ACCEPT

You can REJECT

conclusion that the resurrection of Jesus Christ is one of the "most wicked, vicious, heartless hoaxes" ever foisted upon the minds of men, or it is the most fantastic fact of history.[8]

We each have to choose for ourselves which possibility is the truth.

Pascal's Wager

Blaise Pascal was a mathematician, but some of his friends were into gambling. So he came up with a way of explaining the gospel in language they could understand: He asked them to make a bet.

"God is, or He is not," Pascal said. "But to which side shall we incline? Reason can decide nothing here.... What will you wager?"

Pascal said that he was betting his life on the assumption that God existed. If he was wrong, what had he lost? On the other hand, if he was right, he would gain everything. His friends were gambling that God did not exist. If they were right, what had they gained? Nothing. But if they were wrong, they would suffer infinite loss.

	And He *does*...	And He does *not*...
If you wager that God exists	You have infinite gain	You have lost nothing
If you wager that God does not exist	You have infinite loss	You have gained nothing

From Muck to Monkeys to Me?

The question of primary importance is not one of evolution vs. Creation. The question we all need to ask is: Are we here on this earth by accident or by design?

In order for spontaneous generation (evolution) to be possible, the universe would have to be ten to the 10,000,000,000th years old (that's the number one followed by ten million zeros). Today's scientific community now agrees that the universe is only 16–19 billion years old. Because of this discovery they must leave biological evolution in the dust, so to speak.

The Empty Tomb

Did you know that of all the so-called gods of the past, only one tomb lies empty today?

Confucius' tomb:	Occupied
Buddha's tomb:	Occupied
Mohammed's tomb:	Occupied
Jesus' tomb:	Empty!

May I Quote You?

We have collected a few quotes about Christianity from notable figures of history. They make great conversation starters.

66 99 "God is ever before my eyes. I realize His omnipotence and I fear His anger; but I also recognize His love, His compassion, and His tenderness towards His creatures." Wolfgang Amadeus Mozart

66 99 "There is a necessity for a beginning to the creation of the universe, as well as the presence of a superior reasoning power." Albert Einstein

66 99 "It may be stated categorically that no archaeological discovery has ever disputed a Biblical reference." Jewish archaeologist Nelson Glueck

66 99 "Painting nor sculpture now can lull to rest. My soul, that turns to His great love on high, whose arms to clasp us on the cross are spread." Michelangelo

66 99 "There is in the heart of each man a God-shaped vacuum, which cannot be filled by any created thing, but only by God the Creator, made known through Jesus Christ." Blaise Pascal

66 99 "It [the New Testament] lay under my pillow for the four years of my imprisonment. I read it sometimes, and read it to others. With it, I taught one convict to read." Fyodor Dostoevsky

Speak the Truth in Love

Okay, now your quiver's full, right? You're ready to go out and blow people away with your vast knowledge of apologetics. Watch out, skeptics! Atheists, beware!

Just knowing these things will give you confidence and the desire to learn even more. Your faith will grow stronger as you begin to understand the overwhelming amount of evidence there is in support of the most minute details of the Bible.

Another word of warning: God Himself cannot be proven beyond any scientific doubt. (But He can't be disproved, either!) Very few people deny that Jesus actually existed. There is just too much hard, historical evidence—evidence that would be accepted in any court of law. Nor do most people deny that the Bible is a historical document. It's the divine nature of Jesus and the God-breathed nature of Scripture that cannot be established by evidence alone.

You will never argue anyone into the kingdom. Facts will force no one to conclude that Christianity is true. These things will give you an assurance of what you believe, but they may have little effect on your pre-Christian friends. A person's faith and his willingness to give up control of his life will ultimately determine if he decides to become a Christian.

And remember: You're an ambassador, not an invader.

We know a man, Adam, who went out every Sunday looking for people to witness to. He would seek out people he thought he could engage in theological debates. After months of arguments won, Adam realized that he hadn't led a single person to Christ. One day as he was out prowling for another debate, he felt he heard the Lord say to his heart: "It's about the Cross. It's all about the Cross."

We say the same to you. What's important is not winning arguments. What's important is moving pre-Christians one step closer to the foot of the cross.

It's all about the Cross.

1. Dr. Hugh Ross, "The Fingerprint of God" (Orange, Calif.: Promise Publishing, 1989), 137. Dr. Ross has an outstanding apologetics ministry. Reasons to Believe can be reached at P.O. Box 5978, Pasadena, CA., 91117, or at (626) 335–1480. Website: www.reasons.org.

2. Josh McDowell is an expert at handling tough questions about Jesus. Perhaps that's because he once asked most of them himself. He has written many books on apologetics, including the bestselling *Evidence That Demands a Verdict*, an intense book full of historical evidence for the Christian faith. A simpler and more direct focus on a few major issues can be found in his book, *Tough Questions*. We highly recommend both.

3. All four answers are from *Growing Deep in the Christian Life* by Charles R. Swindoll. Copyright 1986, 1995 by Charles R. Swindoll, Inc. Used by permission of Zondervan Publishing House.

4. Flavius, Josephus, *Antiquities XVIII*, 33.

5. John W. Lea, *The Greatest Book in the World* (Philadelphia: n.p., 1929), as quoted in *Evidence That Demands a Verdict* by Josh McDowell.

6. Ibid.

7. C. S. Lewis, *Mere Christianity* (New York: The Macmillan Company, 1952), 40–1.

8. Josh McDowell, *Evidence That Demands a Verdict* (Arrowhead Springs, Calif.: Campus Crusade for Christ International, 1972), 185. See *Evidence That Demands a Verdict* or the pamphlet "The Resurrection—Hoax or History?" for his complete outline.

No More Freaking Out!

Well, you did it!

You made it through a book—gasp!—on witnessing. You have now read everything you need to know about how to talk about Jesus without freaking out. Most importantly, you are gaining the courage and confidence to pass on the Good News to a lost and dying world.

God's will is for everyone to come to know Him personally (1 Timothy 2:4). God will shower us with opportunities to tell others about Him—if we only ask. He's waiting to pour out a revival on His children, but it has to start with you and me.

We challenge you to make a new commitment to God. Take a moment to get on your knees and ask Him to do a new work in your life. Tell Him you are ready and willing to step out of your spiritual comfort zone and look for opportunities to be used in the lives of the pre-Christians around you. Tell Him you are ready to volunteer to be used in the lives of people who are just as you were— headed for destruction. Tell Him you will never again allow yourself to live a safe, mediocre Christian life. Feel free to confess your fears, doubts, and apathy. God can handle it. Ask Him to help you stop yourself from rationalizing away divine appointments.

WARNING: It's too late to go back to your old ways! You now know too much. So step out boldly with renewed faith, excited to see what's in store for you. Every day ask the Lord to use you, stretch you, and change you to be all that He wants you to be. And expect supernatural results!

Once More, with Feeling

Remember that just as living in a garage doesn't make you a car, living as a Christian does not automatically make you a mighty ambassador for Christ. So as a final encouragement for you, let's review how to start your new life as a child of God who is proud to talk about Jesus any day, anytime, anyplace, without ever freaking out.

- **Seek God:** Ask Him to infuse your faith with a new vibrancy. Decide not to compromise your walk with Him in either your personal or professional life.

- **Don't lose hope:** Believe that all your unbelieving friends, family members, and coworkers are pre-Christians.

- **Pray:** Pray daily for the pre-Christians in your life and expect incredible answers to your prayers.

- **Hear their story:** Start learning the stories of the people in your life by asking them questions and then truly listening to their answers.

- **Write your story:** Write out your three-minute testimony, and tell it to anyone who will listen.

- **Memorize His story:** Learn the plan of salvation in a concise, easy-to-deliver manner.

- **Memorize Scripture:** Start with Philemon 6 and the verses in The Bridge.

- **Start a Chickens Anonymous franchise:** Pick a friend to help hold you accountable so that you don't lose the fire that now burns within you. Then get ten friends together and start a ten-week class at your church or home group, like we did. Use this book as your text. Have snacks, pray for each other, and experience a dramatic change.

- **Move out of your comfort zone:** As you share your faith you will gain a full understanding of every good thing you have in Christ (Philemon 6).

- **Expect amazing results!**

Now that's not too hard, is it? We have faith in you! Take a deep breath, ask the Holy Spirit to do great works through you, and then walk confidently into this new season of your life.

Congratulations! You are now officially a mighty warrior attack sheep. And attack sheep don't freak out!

We Want to Hear from You

We would love to receive your three-minute testimony and hear about your experiences. If you're willing, we might include them in future books or use them in class.

If you would like to be included, please contact us at the address below, and we'll send you a release form for you to include with your story. Reading how God has personally and powerfully transformed the lives of so many people could touch the hearts of thousands of searching and discouraged people.

NO FREAKING OUT!
5019 Westpark Drive
Valley Village, CA 91601
E-mail: nofreakingout@aol.com

You Want More?
Recommended Reading

Here are some great resources that will help you learn more about how to talk about Jesus without freaking out. You can get some of them to read yourself; some you may want to give away to your seeking friends.

BOOKS ON WITNESSING AND THE CHRISTIAN LIFE

• *Becoming a Contagious Christian* by Bill Hybels—creative appraches to personal evangelism

• *Evangelizing the New Age* by Paul McGuire—how to witness to people who embrace New Age ideologies

• *Hand Me Another Brick* by Charles Swindoll—a Christian's guide to handling life's struggles, as seen through Nehemiah

• *How Now Shall We Live* by Charles W. Colson—equips Christians to live out and defend their biblical worldview in today's competing worldviews.

• *How to Bring Men to Christ* by R. A. Torrey—how to begin to share your life with nonbelievers

- *Improving Your Serve* by Charles Swindoll—a guide to becoming an effective Christian

- *Jesus Rediscovered* by Malcolm Muggeridge—facts about who Jesus really is

- *Jesus and the Intellectual* by Dr. Bill Bright—an intellectual approach to believing in Jesus Christ

- *Life Together* by Dietrich Bonhoeffer—a look at what a Christian life is truly about, written by a theologian who was assassinated on Hitler's orders

- *Mere Christianity* by C. S. Lewis—an intellectual look at Christianity

- *More Than a Carpenter* by Josh McDowell—an insight into who Jesus was and is

- *Out of the Salt Saker and into the World* by Rebecca Manley Pippert—evangelism as a way of life

- *Tell It Often, Tell It Well* by Mark McCloskey—making the most of witnessing opportunities

- *When God Doesn't Make Sense* by Dr. James Dobson—a great book for dealing with tough questions about pain and suffering

- *Witnessing without Fear* by Dr. Bill Bright—a confidence builder and how-to guide to share your faith in Christ

TESTIMONIAL BOOKS

- *Betrayed* by Stan Telchen—the testimony of a Jew struggling with his daughter's new faith in Christ

- *Ben Israel* by Arthur Katz—the personal testimony of a Jewish man who became a Christian

- *Death of a Guru* by Rabi Maharaj—the conversion of a Hindu guru to Christianity

- *Jesus, Hollywood, and Me* by Al Kasha—the story of a two-time Academy Award winning composer who became a Christian and was delivered from agoraphobia

- *Lion and Lamb* by Brennan Manning—the testimony of a devout Catholic who became a born-again believer

- *The Case for Christ* by Lee Strobel—a journalist's personal investigation of the evidence for Jesus

- *Welcome all Wonders* by J.A.C. Redford—a composer's journey out of Mormonism and into Christianity

BOOKS ON APOLOGETICS

- *Answers to Tough Questions* by Josh McDowell and Don Stewart—answers to difficult questions about God

- *Can Man Live without God?* by Ravi Zacharias—a compelling apologetic defense of the Christian faith

- *Evidence That Demands a Verdict and More Evidence That Demands a Verdict* by Josh McDowell—historical facts proving the validity of the Bible

- *Reasons Why Skeptics Should Consider Christianity* by Josh McDowell and Don Stewart—answers to tough questions often asked by skeptics

- *The Creator of the Cosmos* by Hugh Ross—scientific facts proving the validity of the Bible

• *The Resurrection Factor* by Josh McDowell—historical evidence supporting the resurrection of Jesus Christ

ADDITIONAL APOLOGETICS RESOURCES

Much of the information we compiled for chapter 11 came from the following resources:

• REASONS TO BELIEVE is an international, interdenominational ministry established to communicate the scientific truths, discoveries, and principles that are the basis for believing the Bible is the wholly true Word of God. Web site: www.reasons.org. Address: P.O. Box 5978, Pasadena, CA 91117. Phone: (626) 335-1480.

• JOSH MCDOWELL MINISTRIES is an international evangelistic ministry committed to telling the world the truth. You can reach them at P.O. Box 131000, Dallas, Texas 75313, or visit their web site at www.josh.org.

• CHARLES SWINDOLL, P.O. Box 69000, Anaheim, CA 92817-0900. For more information about his ministry, call (800) 772-8888 or check their web site at www.insight.org.

A Letter about Jesus

Over the years, we have written letters to pre-Christians to explain the gospel to them. We include one to give you an example of this approach to witnessing. If you would like to purchase duplicates to hand out as tracts, please contact us at the address on the "We Want to Hear from You," page 232.

From Karen to Sam

This is the letter I wrote to Sam after I sat next to him on an airplane and failed to say what I wanted to about God and Sam's need to know Jesus (see chapter 1).

Dear Sam,

I very much enjoyed our talk on the plane last Friday. However, I am finding the need to write to you to clarify a few of the things that I said that disturbed me. I have thought about our talk and believe that I should have challenged you on a couple of points. I want to give you an alternative point of view to ponder. I also have to stand firm on what I so deeply believe instead of taking the easy way out in order to avoid conflict.

Therefore, I ask that you read this knowing that I am driven by my love for God and my concern for your well-being. (Why? I don't know, other than your pain touched my heart and your need for fulfillment touched my soul.)

God can and does speak to us through giving us a "peace" or "joy." However, He will never give us a feeling that contradicts the Scriptures. The Bible is the "Word of God." It is God-breathed, and He has spoken through righteous men to give us this guidebook. Therefore, we either believe all of it or none of it. Picking and choosing what we want to believe negates the truthfulness of both the Bible and of God Himself. And if God is not absolute truth, there is no moral standard from which man can decide what is wrong and what is right.

You are a very smart man, so I believe that you will believe me when I say that God loves His people. He loves you very much and He wants you to be happy—even more than you do! Therefore, the path to ultimate joy and fulfillment is to seek Him, learn about Him, read His Book, struggle with His laws and embrace His commandments. The joy we get solely from other people is very short-term. The joy God offers us is forever, and it includes incredible relationships with people that He brings into our lives. Only through God can you get the "love of your life."

I am assuming, of course, that we are talking about the same God. I am not talking about a higher power, an energy source, a light within us, or even the man upstairs. I am talking about the almighty God, the Creator of the universe, the Alpha and the Omega, Yahweh, the great I AM. There is only one true God and all others are false gods. He is the

God of the Bible and the only true source of power, unconditional love, absolute truth, and total forgiveness. He is the God you need to seek out and find.

Secondly, there is a part of God that your rabbi probably won't tell you about. It is the part He sent down to earth to personalize the laws He taught us in the Old Testament. That is the Son of God, the part of the Creator God that is both God and Man in the person of Jesus. He is a difficult part of God for Jews to embrace—not because of the Scriptures, for there are hundreds of prophecies about Him in the Old Testament, but because of the events of human history beginning, interestingly enough, the day Jesus came to earth as a newborn babe. If you can read about Jesus the Messiah in both the Old Testament and the New Testament not as a cultural Jew, but as a man seeking God, you will see that Jesus truly poses no threat to you at all. He is only a part of God, coming down in the flesh, to tell all of us that He loves us. He wants us to live abundant, fulfilling lives on earth, and He wants to offer us the gift of eternal life in heaven.

That's all great stuff for us. He Himself even made it clear that He actually came FIRST to the Jew and then to the non-Jew. You truly are His chosen people. I have included a book that I give you as a gift in your spiritual and personal journey (*Betrayed* by Stan Telchin). I continue to pray that you read the Bible, and you may always call me or my husband at the number on my card. Thanks for reading.

Karen Covell

The Purposes of Fasting with Prayer

The following is taken from Bill Bright's book, *The Transforming Power of Fasting and Prayer.* We put it here to help you evaluate fasting as a spiritual discipline.[1] We ask that you prayerfully consider these purposes in fasting:

- to honor God (*Matthew 6:16–18; Zechariah 7:5; Luke 2:37; Acts 13:2*);

- to humble ourselves before God (*Ezra 8:21; Psalm 69:10; Isaiah 58:3*);

- to experience more grace (*1 Peter 5:5*) and God's intimate presence (*Isaiah 57:15; 58:6–9*);

- to mourn over personal sin and failure (*1 Samuel 7:6; Nehemiah 9:1–2*);

- to mourn over the sins of the church, nation, and world (*1 Samuel 7:6; Nehemiah 9:1–2*);

- to seek grace for a new task, for the work God has sent us to do, and to reaffirm our consecration to God (*Matthew 4:2*);

- to seek God by drawing near to Him and persisting in prayer against opposing spiritual forces (*Judges 20:26; Ezra 8:21, 23, 31; Jeremiah 29:12–14; Joel 2:12; Luke 18:3; Acts 9:10–19*);

- to show repentance and so make a way for God to change His declared intentions of judgment (*2 Samuel 12:16, 22; 1 Kings 21:27–29; Jeremiah 18:7–8; Joel 2:12–14; Jonah 3:5–10*);

- to save people from bondage to evil (*Isaiah 58:6; Matthew 17:14–21; Luke 4:1*);

- to gain revelation and wisdom concerning God's will (*Isaiah 58:5, 6, 11; Daniel (3 17–18, 21–22; Acts 13:2, 3*);

- to open the way for the outpouring of the Spirit and Christ's return to earth for His people (*Matthew 9:15; 25:6; John 14:3*).

1. Dr. Bill Bright, *The Transforming Power of Fasting and Prayer* (Orlando, Fla.: New Life Publications, 1997). Also read *The Coming Revival* and *Preparing for the Coming Revival,* both by Bill Bright (Orlando, Fla.: New Life Publications, 1995). For more information, contact Campus Crusade for Christ, P.O. Box 593684, Orlando, FL 32859 or e-mail to CompuServe: 74114,1206 or e-mail them at newlife@magicnet.net.